Successful Praying

F. J. HUEGEL

Successful Praying

DIMENSION BOOKS
BETHANY FELLOWSHIP, INC.
MINNEAPOLIS, MINNESOTA

Printed in the United States of America

To the memory of
PRAYING HYDE
of India

CONTENTS

Chapter I

IT HAS OFTEN BEEN SAID that prayer is the greatest force in the universe. This is no exaggeration. It will bear constant repetition. In this atomic age when forces are being released that stagger the thought and imagination of man, it is well to remember that prayer transcends all other forces.

The reason lies near at hand. It is that prayer does not release some mere force of man or nature. Prayer releases the immeasurable wealth and power of Almighty God. "Call unto me, and I will answer thee, and shew thee great and mighty things, which thou knowest not" (Jer. 33:3). There you have it. "*I* will shew you great and mighty things." It is the voice of God. It is the omnipotent Sovereign, Creator and Sustainer of a hundred million universes, as astronomers are wont to speak of creation today, who here gives us His Word. He says, in effect, that if you will pray He will work. He with whom nothing is impossible, who spoke and worlds without number came into being, pledges His most holy and immutable word that if we will but seek His face in prayer He will work and bring to pass great and mighty things such as have never been entertained in the mind and thought of man.

It is to be understood that the great and mighty things which the Lord of heaven and earth promises to bring to pass are those which have to do with the well-being of the children of men. The Lord is bent on the redemption of mankind. To attain this end He threw in, as it were, everything He had. He spared not His own Son but delivered him up for us all. He gave what was dearer than a million worlds. God's supreme purpose has as its goal the everlasting bliss of the children of men. That is why He gave Himself in the person of His only Son, the Beloved of the Father, to die in infinite shame and pain upon a wretched Cross that sin, the enthralling monster, enemy of man's well-being and happiness, might be forever destroyed. That Christ the Redeemer might be enthroned in the hearts of men and His Kingdom established, God will work great and mighty things in answer to the prayers of His children.

It is an amazing thing that should stab Christians into an awful realization of their responsibility, that in a real sense God has limited Himself in the working of the great and mighty things He so desires to accomplish for man's good, to the prayers of His people. If we will not pray, to put it bluntly, He cannot work. Jesus our Lord, we are told, could not do the mighty works of love and healing He was wont to do, in Nazareth, His home town. It was because of the unbelief of the people. Unbelief and prayerlessness spring from the same root. As unbelief bound the Saviour's hands, so prayerlessness binds God's. Just why God's working the great and mighty things for man's eternal well-being and glory is limited to man's praying may be one of the deep mysteries of theology, but there it stands. If there is a fact to which the Bible, which has been called a textbook on prayer, bears eloquent witness, it is this fact. If there is one thing that stands out with letters aflame with meaning, it is that if God is to work great and mighty things in the affairs of men and nations, carrying forward His sublime purposes of redemption, men must pray, lifting their voices to the throne of God in earnest supplication and sincere adoration. They must pray as did Abraham, pray as did Jacob, pray as did Moses, pray as did Isaiah and the prophets, yea, pray as did Jesus our Lord and His apostles.

We would not minimize the importance of other forms of service in the establishment of the Kingdom of God. But we must admit that prayer is the foremost weapon ("The weapons of our warfare are not carnal, but mighty through God"). Prayer must undergird all forms of Christian service if they are to be truly fruitful. You can do good things and bless men without prayer; but God's ends wherein man's eternal good is found, cannot be so achieved. We see an example in the life of our Lord. As a man He wrought nothing without prayer. He initiated nothing without prayerfully waiting on the Father. He laid down an unvarying principle, saying, "The Son can do nothing of himself, but what he seeth the Father do" (John 5:19). Prayer with the Son of Man was as the very breath of life. "Father," He said, as He stood beside Lazarus' tomb, "I thank thee that thou hast heard me. And I knew that thou hearest me always." His closing word on the Cross was a prayer. We are told that He ever liveth to make intercession for us.

Prayer is not only man's highest privilege and his most cherished joy (for thereby he holds communion with Him who is the Fountain of Life), but it is also man's most effective weapon whereby he may achieve. Beside this all else pales as when the stars are eclipsed by the rising sun. All else leaves man floundering in the muck and chaos of self-effort which has never been anything but a blind alley. All else leaves him as a frail bark on life's stormy seas without a helm, without a compass, without a pilot. If we build without direction from the Most High who orders all for man's good according to an eternal plan (here is the highest definition of prayer whereby we listen to God and receive strength to obey), our labors, however brilliant, must finally come to naught. It is he who doeth the will of

God who abideth forever (I John 2:17). Prayer in its truest form, its deepest and most worthy expression, brings man's little day and effort into a harmonious blend with the great pattern and purposes of the Father of Lights and thereby gives to man's otherwise puny achievements everlasting glory and meaning.

Prayer is work of such a sublime order that it lies beyond the imagination of men. For when the Christian prays, his capacity to achieve and his power to do good are multiplied a thousand, yea, a hundred thousandfold. This is no exaggeration, the reason being that when man prays, God works. It is now no longer mere man, though without man's co-operation the vast machine of spiritual outreach and achievement is, so to speak, without a spark plug. It is man releasing the wealth of the bank of heaven. It is man confounding himself with the purposes of God and so making it possible for them to be realized. It is man plus God. Oh, what a plus! Nay, it is God releasing his matchless energies in lieu of a decisive factor without which Omnipotence is in a sense rendered impotent. Witness Moses standing in the breach and praying for forgiveness for the children of Israel when, because of the worship of the golden calf, the Lord's wrath was kindled and He purposed to destroy Israel. Listen to the voice of God as He speaks saying (Ezek. 22:30, 31), "And I sought for a man among them, that should make up the hedge, and stand in the gap before me for the land, that I should not destroy it: but I found none. Therefore I have poured out mine indignation upon them; I have consumed them with the fire of my wrath. . . ." Witness the ministry of prayer of the great intercessors of the Bible. Witness the achievements of the George Müllers and the Praying Hydes and the David Brainerds and the Amy Carmichaels of the Church.

One might open the Book of the Psalms almost at random and find such passages as this one:

"Fools because of their transgression, and because of their iniquities, are afflicted. Their soul abhorreth all manner of meat; and they draw near unto the gates of death. Then they cry unto the Lord in their trouble, and he saveth them out of their distresses. He sent his word, and healed them, and delivered them from their destructions. Oh that men would praise the Lord for his goodness, and for his wonderful works to the children of men!" (Ps. 107:17-21)

The power of prayer is shown forcibly in the words which President Eisenhower chose as his text on the day of his inauguration. "If my people, which are called by my name, shall humble themselves, and pray, and seek my face, and turn from their wicked ways; then will I hear from heaven, and will forgive their sin, and will heal their land" (II Chron. 7:14).

Furthermore, when man prays, he is no longer hemmed in within the circle of a merely human sphere of activity. His tiny scope as he seeks to do good and to bless benighted souls in need of the redemptive liberation of the Gospel of Christ, becomes as vast as the life of the nations. When he preaches, should he be a herald of the glad tidings of God's love, he may bless a congregation of believers; but when he prays his capacity to bless is without limit. He may pray, as he is admonished to do, for all the saints and consequently bless a hundred million believers, yea, all the members of the body of Christ. It is no longer he (though he be indispensable) but the One who sustains the universe and gives to all things their virtue and whose power to bless knows no bounds. Through prayer you can touch the ends of the earth and enter upon a universal ministry. Prayer makes it possible for you to open a beneficent and immeasurably bountiful hand to bless souls in distant lands. Through prayer you may release forces which will bring redemption to races cursed with cannibalism and idolatry and superstition and despair in continents beyond the seas. What a staggering fact. Jesus our Lord in His high priestly prayer prayed for all those who should believe on Him (John 17:20). His prayer embraced the ages. So yours may bless peoples yet unborn. On your knees you may thrust forth missionaries to the farthermost reaches of a sin-stricken humanity's heathenism; you may visit every prison in America and be a bearer of light to souls that secretly weep in the throes of endless night; you may visit every brothel in all the cities of the world and snatch souls from the flames of everlasting shame and bring them to the One who forgave all to the woman who kissed His sacred feet and washed them with her tears. Lest you think I am indulging in mad hyperboles, please read what the Saviour says in Luke 10:2, and John 15:7. With God neither time nor space are barriers. He can work immediately in the hearts of men everywhere. Did not the Saviour say, speaking of the coming of the Holy Spirit, that He would convict the world of sin? And are we not given to understand that it is not the Father's will for any to perish? And is it not written that he (Christ the Lord) is the propitiation for the sins of the whole world? (I John 2:2)

It is when men bow the knee and call upon God that in a sense they become as mighty as the Almighty. Do not misunderstand me. I am not being irreverent. I am only saying what He says in His Holy Word. "Call unto me, and I will answer thee, and shew thee great and mighty things, which thou knowest not." You pray, says the Almighty God, and I will work. If you ask anything in my name, I will do it. "And call upon me in the day of trouble: I will deliver thee, and thou shalt glorify me" (Ps. 50:15).

Come, He says in effect, bow the knee and call upon me. As you pray I will work. I pledge my omnipotence. You may not see at once any change, though there are times when before my people call, I answer. If you will but believe and wait upon me, all things will be possible; the very course of history may be changed, for with me nothing is impossible.

Again I quote the words of Holy Writ where the Lord says: "I sought for a man among them that should make up the hedge, and stand in the gap before me for the land, that I should not destroy it: but I found none. Therefore I have poured out mine indignation upon them; I have consumed them with the fire of my wrath: their own way have I recompensed upon their heads, saith the Lord" (Ezek. 22:30, 31).

Chapter II

WE HAVE SAID THAT THE GREATEST FORCE in the universe is prayer. Almighty God gives His Word in a solemn pledge that He will work if man will only pray. But He does not make "exceeding great and precious promises" without stipulating in most concise fashion the conditions which must prevail on the human side if the results of prayer are to be commensurate with the promise.

James says we have not because we ask not. It *is* that simple. He then goes on to say that we ask and receive not because we ask amiss, whereby we are given to understand that the matter is not so simple after all. In other words, prayer as everything else, has its laws which must be taken into account. There is not in all the material universe a phenomenon that is not governed by law. It is no less true in the world of the spirit as Drummond pointed out years ago in his epochal work, *Natural Law in the Spiritual World*. Though not spoken of as such, these laws are all found in the Bible. The Word is our infallible guide.

The most basic of these laws which govern prayer is the law of the Atonement; the foundation not only of the Christian life but of prayer which springs from that life. It is simple. It is not an intricate theological question grasped by only a few. Here you have it: No man can come into the presence of God and expect an audience standing on the ground of his own merits. His own righteousness will not avail. We have the authority of Scripture that in God's sight man's righteousness is but a filthy rag. Nothing that man can do will make him acceptable to God. The havoc wrought by sin is too tragic and too fatal for that. We must be emphatic about this for there is much glib and alluring talk about prayer abroad today which would have us think and believe otherwise. This, the most basic law of prayer, is by-passed. The Cross is spurned. The blood of the Atonement is counted an unholy thing. Satan has shown his hand here though to be sure he would fain hide it. Prayer on any other basis than Calvary is a satanic counterfeit for it is still a fact according to Christ's own avowed affirmation that no man can come to the Father but by Him.

We enter into the holiest by the blood of Jesus, by a new and living way which He hath consecrated for us, through the veil, that is to say, His flesh (Heb. 10:19, 20). He is the door: He has been made unto us wisdom and righteousness and sanctification and redemption, and it is only as by faith we appropriate Him, that we are acceptable unto the Father. Nor does that mean that to give prayer its proper form we must close with the accustomed, "In Jesus' Name." It goes deeper than that as we shall see. Still, if we would stand before the Father on unshakeable ground which can never be questioned — ground provided by God Himself, ground which not only satisfies Him but also man who without the cleansing provided at Calvary could never find the courage or the faith to face a Holy God whom he has so bitterly offended — it must be the rock-bottom foundation of the Cross.

There are many ways of stating the most amazing fact of the universe. Our Blessed Redeemer bore our sin in His body on the Tree. He who knew no sin was made sin for us that we might be made the righteousness of God in Him. God was in Christ reconciling the world unto Himself. We draw near to God in full assurance of faith because of our great High Priest who, when He had by

Himself purged our sins, sat down on the right hand of the Majesty on high. We must wash our garments, as it is written in the Apocalypse, and make them white in the Blood of the Lamb. So reads Holy Writ.

Now if on any other ground, as so much of the religious lore of the hour seems to indicate, we could draw near to God, the Father would betray the Son who at so great a cost of pain and shame and ignominy and torture and death poured out the last drop of His precious blood on Calvary's awful Cross that man's sin might be blotted out. He that honoreth not the Son honoreth not the Father who sent Him. Come, let us be honest about this matter lest we be deceived by the enemy. There is nowhere that he practices with such subtlety his astute machinations as in the matter of prayer. We simply have no leg on which to stand, no firm ground of hope, no certain way of approach to a Holy God unless it be that provided by the Lamb of God who taketh away the sin of the world.

It is an awful thing to draw near to God. The Israelites trembled and could not endure the manifestations of the presence of God in the Holy Mount and even Moses did fear and quake. The truth of the matter is that the sinner flees from the presence of God and hides in terror. Fear grips his heart and as he looks upon his garments so besmirched by sin and recalls the times without number that he has violated God's laws and spurned His love, he realizes that he could no more enter God's presence than a thug could enter the presence of a banker whose vaults he had just looted.

Ah, but when one looks at Calvary and sees the Saviour bearing his sins, then it is that an illimitable confidence surges in one's breast and it becomes easy to lay hold of God in prayer, believing that what is asked for shall be given. Prayer on the ground of Calvary where God and man meet, the law which demands the death of the sinner having exhausted itself in the execution of the Son of God (Son of Man), may become a cosmic affair illimitable in scope and power. Not long ago I had an experience which brought all this home to my heart in irresistible fashion. I was called to the British-American hospital to see a lady I had known when she was a happy girl forever bubbling over with mirth. There she lay paralyzed from her head to the tip of her toes. She whispered to me saying it was not polio, and that the doctors did not know what it was. After a brief visit I offered prayer that the Lord might heal her. As I left the hospital I felt that the Lord chided me, saying I had gone too fast and had failed to grasp the meaning of the situation. I asked to be forgiven and hurried home.

Some days later I returned to see how this suffering soul was doing. There was no change in her condition. As I sat at her bedside I prayed for light to know how to proceed. It came in a flash. I observed that the patient was willing enough for me to talk about the love of God but that the moment any mention was made of the Cross of Christ as the ground of a sinner's approach to God, a strange look, one of utter rebellion and unbelief, came into her eyes. Any reference to the blood of Christ, which cleanseth from all sin, seemed to shake her paralyzed body with a satanic defiance. As I left the hospital I thanked God for showing me where and how the fight would have to be waged. As I walked down the street on my way home, I took a stand in my spirit against the enemy and in the Name of Jesus and on the basis of the victory won on Calvary, I claimed release from the powers of darkness for this dear one. Peace came to my heart for I knew that the Lord had given me the key to the situation and that all would soon be well.

Upon returning a few days later I found a great change in the patient; I do not mean physically, but spiritually. I could now talk about the Saviour who bore our sins in His body on the tree, and of how He reconciled us to the Father through the shedding of His precious blood on Calvary's Cross. The heart's door was open. I was able to enter and tell of a crucified, resurrected Saviour by whose stripes we are healed. I left the hospital rejoicing, little doubting that this change would speedily reach the physical aspect of the matter, too.

A week later I returned to find the patient with the blood red glow of health in her face as she exercised her limbs under the bed covers with unutterable glee. There was nothing to do but praise God from whom all blessings flow. When a week later I called again the nurse informed me that the patient was healed and had returned to her home. A year later I received a letter from this dear one telling me that a baby had come to the home and that she had the unspeakable joy of motherhood. Indeed, it is when we come to the Father in the Name of His dearly beloved Son who bore our sins in His body on the Tree, and whose precious blood cleanseth from all sin, that we may be bold in making known our requests and be confident that exceeding abundant above all that we could think of or ask for shall be given.

Perhaps the most classic expression in all Christian literature of this matter of our approach to God through our Mediator, Jesus Christ the Lord, who by the blood of His Cross wrought redemption, is found in Amy Carmichael's book, *Rose from Brier*, where she breaks forth in poetic fashion saying:

> Lord, is all well? Oh, tell me; is all well?
>> No voice of man can reassure the soul
>> When over it the waves and billows roll:
> His words are like the tinkling of a bell
>> Do *Thou* speak: is all well?

Across the turmoil of the wind and sea,
But as it seemed from somewhere near to me,
A voice I know — "Child look at Calvary:
By the merits of my blood all is well."

Whence came the voice? Lo, He is in the boat:
Lord, wert Thou resting in Thy love when I,
Faithless and fearful, broke into that cry?
O Lord, forgive; a shell would keep afloat
Didst thou make it Thy boat.

And now I hear Thy mighty "Peace, be still,"
And wind and wave are calm, their fury, froth,
And could wind or wave cause Thee to break Thy troth?
They are but servants to Thy sovereign will;
Within me all is still.

Oh, was there ever light on land or sea,
Or ever sweetness of the morning air,
Or ever clear blue gladness anywhere
Like this that flows from Love on Calvary
From Him who stilled the sea?

Father and Son and Spirit be adored;
Father who gave to death our Blessed Lord;
Spirit who speaks through the Eternal Word,
By the merits of the Blood all is well.

To PRAY IN THE NAME WHICH IS ABOVE EVERY NAME, the Name of Jesus our Lord, does not only mean to pray on the ground of the Atonement. It means that, but it means more. We are not simply reconciled to the Father by the blood of the Redeemer's Cross. We are brought by the same Cross into a glorious position before the Father. The teaching of the Word is that in lieu of the Saviour's identification with the children of men — bone of their bone, flesh of their flesh, tempted in all points like as they, in truth and indeed the Son of Man — what befell Him as man's great Representative, the Second Adam, befell man. He was crucified, then man was crucified, "the old man," together with Him (Rom. 6:6). He died, then all died (II Cor. 5:14, RSV). He was buried, we also were buried in the likeness of his death (Rom. 6:5). He arose — with Him we arose (Eph. 2:4,5). He ascended and is seated at the right hand of the Father. We, too, are in this same position of ascendency, seated in heavenly places with Christ our Lord (Eph. 2:6).

Now to fail to take into account the plain teaching of the Scriptures regarding the exalted position of the Christian as co-heir (Rom. 8:17) with Christ, as seems to be the case with many books on prayer, cuts the central nerve of this most holy function, robbing prayer in a large measure of its efficacy. We would not attempt to come into the presence of some high earthly magistrate and seek an audience without taking into account the established order of procedure, much less in our approach to God. If as a Christian I assume the groveling attitude of a beggar when all the time the Heavenly Father bids me bear in mind that I have been made a king and a priest unto Him in Christ, sharing His death and His resurrection, seated with Him in heavenly places, I shall most certainly find myself at cross purposes with Him and prayer is to no small degree stripped of its rightful power. True, one must be humble, but a feigned humility, however sincerely manifested, is of no avail. It must be a humility wrought into the deepest fabric of my being, natural and unfeigned, as a result of my oneness with the Saviour whose "death — resurrection — mid-process" I share, old things having passed away and all things having become new.

All this has a profound bearing on prayer. Prayer can only be effective in its highest Biblical sense — the prayer of the righteous man which availeth much — as it springs from the "new creation," the old having come to an end in the Cross. The "old man," however religious he may be, cannot in the truest sense of the word, pray. He cannot hold communion with God. The "carnal mind," which according to Romans 8:7, is at enmity with God, cannot approach Him in an acceptable way. It is under the verdict of the Cross. It was put out of God's sight "judicially" at Calvary. A lion may be tamed, but he is still a lion, and some sudden change of circumstances may arouse the beast.

The "flesh" (as we have it in the overwhelming picture given to us in Galatians 5, where not only are there obscene and loathsome things which one blushes to mention, but also things which in the church's life pass as quite innocent if not commendable, such as rivalries, divisions and strife) is, however polished with religious zeal, still "flesh" and can never be anything else. God cannot look upon it.

Christians, Paul tells us, have crucified it. Now if I pray, let us say, for revival in my church (and where is the church that does not need revival) from a sectarian position with sectional, denominational rivalry as the secret motive, it takes no profound discernment to see that I am at cross purposes with God and grieve Him even as I call upon Him. I must "die" before I can properly pray. I must enter into an ever deeper participation in the Cross if the heinous "self-life" with its lust for praise, "the flesh" with its greed for the limelight of religious publicity, "the old man" with his self-infatuation, are to be kept from nullifying the effectiveness of my prayers. How much of the travail of God's people as they pray for the great work of the church comes to naught because the deeper aspects of the Cross are not allowed to operate!

A pastor was given a dream in which he heard the voice of the Lord who asked him to take an invoice of the motives which dominated his ministry. The revelation overwhelmed him with shame. It was found as the Spirit of God searched the hidden springs of his being that something like thirty per cent must be charged to sectarian pride, thirty per cent to vainglory over oratorical achievements, twenty per cent went to ecclesiastical bigotry, social position and family pride. When the count was over a measly five per cent remained of actual love for God and genuine zeal for His glory and honor. Now to really pray as did Paul and the great peers of the church down the ages, as did Knox who cried, "Lord, give me Scotland or I die," as did Praying Hyde who through his groans and tears and intercessions brought revival to India, there must be an application of the Cross by the Holy Spirit to the innermost citadels of the "self-life," so that "the new creation" in the power of Christ's resurrection which alone has a bona fide, gilt-edge claim on the things of God, may exercise its power.

Here is where much praying for what is called "a baptism of power," comes to naught. God dare not answer prayer for power, power from on high, which springs from wrong motives. The oil, as we read in Leviticus, was not applied to the flesh. The Father cannot give power to that which in Christ He put to death. Power given to the "old creation," far from promoting the interests of the Kingdom of God, would only be material for Satan to exploit in the interests of the kingdom which he rules. The Holy Spirit cannot entrust the servants of the Church with the treasures of Pentecost until He has led them to a vital experience of the deeper implications of Calvary as they are set forth in Romans six.

Furthermore, when a Christian's prayer life springs from a right position (a thorough adjustment to Christ in His death and resurrection), a vast change in procedure follows. Much of the mere begging type (though of course asking is always in order for the Lord says, "Ask and ye shall receive") gives way to a positive and unspeakably joyous appropriation. Much of our begging fails to register in heaven because it fails to spring from right relations with the Father in union with Christ in death and resurrection; in which position one simply appropriates what is already his. "All things," says the apostle, "are yours, for ye are Christ's and Christ is God's."

When I stand by faith in the position, for example, assigned to me in Colossians 3:3, where it is written: ". . . ye are dead, and your life is hid with Christ in God" (the judicial standing of all Christians), my prayer life takes on a totally different character. Such a position sets me apart and in truth takes me where Christ Himself is, makes me a co-heir of God with Him and invests me with an authority and a glory like Christ's. It could not be otherwise. Even in the days of His flesh before the consummation of Calvary and the resurrection with Pentecost following, the

Saviour was wont to hint at the glories which were to come for the believer. He said in effect, "If ye say to this mountain, be thou removed and doubt not in your heart, what ye say shall be done." We often plead for the removal of some mountain of oppression and difficulty when what God expects of us is the command of faith, speaking directly to the prince of darkness and as those who sit with Jesus in heavenly places, claiming the destruction of His works: When we do this the mountain disappears. We may have to wait some times to actually "see" what was commanded in naked faith. But if we doubt not, we shall at last *see* what *faith without any evidence of the senses simply took.*

In this position of oneness with Christ the Lord in His exaltation where we "reign in life by one, Jesus Christ" (Rom. 5), praise takes the place of petition. Not that petition altogether ceases. We still ask and receive. But now we properly measure our riches. The measure of our riches is the measure of the riches of our royal Brother. We are one with Him. He is our life. His death is our death; His resurrection our resurrection; His exaltation our exaltation. Where the Head is, the body is also found. As the body finds in the Head its joy and crown, so the Head finds in the body its fulfillment (see Eph. 1:22, 23).

In the light of these facts the believer needs much time for praise. And as he sings and rejoices and praises, he finds to his infinite delight that God works and His promises become real in actual experience. "Delight thyself also in the Lord; and he shall give thee the desires of thine heart" (Ps. 37:4). Throughout all eternity we will be praising God for our inheritance in Christ, so let us lose no time, let us begin now. Let us by faith embrace all the implications of the Cross the Holy Spirit would apply, and in a new freedom we will pray from the lofty position of "the new creation."

Chapter IV

It would seem at first quite unnecessary to speak of the need of faith in relation to prayer. Would one pray if one did not believe in God's willingness to hear and answer? In actual practice, however, we find that there is often much prayer with little or no faith that prayer will be heard and answered. The truth of the matter is that it is easier to pray than it is to believe. The reason is to be found in the fact that prayer is the human side of the matter, while faith puts it over on the divine side. We all by nature (I do not say by grace; grace is another matter) have a high regard for our own doing, whereas we are blind to the operations of God. Furthermore, faith is in proportion to our obedience and the purity of our lives and motives. John in his first Epistle states it in this fashion: "If our heart condemn us not, then have we confidence toward God," the inference being that if our hearts condemn us, we just cannot work up real confidence.

So we are driven back to the first law of prayer: the Atonement. The moment we get our eyes off Calvary real faith goes by the board. It is only as we see our way clear to a satisfactory straightening out of our accounts before God (and how can that ever be apart from the Cross where our sins were dealt with and put away forever) that we are in a position to come boldly before the throne of grace with the burning requests of our hearts.

Faith comes quite naturally to one who is walking in the

pathway of obedience to his Lord and is enjoying His ungrieved presence. We read in I Corinthians twelve, where we have that most classic passage on the working of the Holy Spirit and the gifts He imparts to believers, that it is He who inspires faith, which does not mean that cooperation on the human side is not necessary, for it is man who is commanded to exercise faith and with him it must begin. In the heart of one who is filled with the Spirit, faith is as natural and as unconscious as breathing. It is because we have received the Spirit of adoption that we cry Abba, Father (see Rom. 8:15). If the Spirit is quenched then prayer is quenched. Indeed, faith has its laws. We do not believe by sheer force of will, though there is such a thing as the will to believe, as William James, America's foremost philosopher and father of pragmatism, used to say.

Faith, Paul tells us, comes by hearing, and hearing by the Word of God. If I may only find the right words — the promise in Holy Writ which will fit the need as a key fits a lock for which it is made — then faith in the hour of prayer is given a sure footing and great things will be wrought. I shall soon be singing the glad song of victory even as Moses and Joshua and David and Paul and the galaxy of Old and New Testament saints were wont to sing as they saw the arm of God laid bare in answer to prayer.

We must indeed believe that God is a rewarder of them that diligently seek Him. Prayer without faith is a mockery. Listen to the voice of Jesus as He speaks saying: "Therefore I say unto you, What things soever ye desire, when ye pray, believe that ye receive them, and ye shall have them" (Mark 11:24). We must ask in faith, writes James, nothing wavering. If he is tossed about as a wave of the sea, "let not that man think he shall receive any thing of the Lord" (Jas. 1:7).

The Saviour declared that all things are possible to him that believeth. We are wont to think of such potency as attributed to faith in terms of hyperbole, if not gross exaggeration. But our Lord was not indulging in poetic license, nor were the words of Him who is the Truth ever those of an extremist. "Have faith in God. For verily I say unto you, That whosoever shall say unto this mountain, Be thou removed, and be thou cast into the sea; and shall not doubt in his heart, but shall believe that those things which he saith shall come to pass; he shall have whatsoever he saith" (Mark 11:22, 23). But the Saviour is not simply talking about faith *in* God. The Greek brings out the thought of the faith *of* God. Paul seems to have had this in mind in that passionate cry which is the quintessence of the Gospel: "I am crucified with Christ; nevertheless I live; yet not I, but Christ liveth in me: and the life which I now live in the flesh, I live by the faith of the Son of God, who loved me and gave himself for me." It is the faith of the Son of God. He could not dwell by His Spirit within our hearts without being not only our humility, our love, our patience, our righteousness, but our very life, and that means our very faith.

When it is the faith of the Son of God which rises within the Christian's breast in the hour of prayer, not only are mountains of difficulty removed, but miracles such as Jesus our Lord brought to pass are wrought. He said to his disciples that they would do greater works than those which He had wrought. That need not shock us. Greater works are wrought but it is still the Lord working through His disciples. It is "the faith of the Son of God." Greater works because Calvary is now the ground of our praying. Calvary and the empty tomb and Pentecost make possible for the believer what was not yet possible in the days when Jesus our Lord walked in Galilee.

Indeed we must not doubt in our hearts as we seek the Father's face in prayer; nor is it possible to doubt when in union with Christ we lay hold of the promise. Ours is "the faith of the Son of God," not something worked up in the strength of the natural, but an overflowing joy, a certitude which surges within as we stand united with our Lord in the power of His resurrection (Phil. 3:10).

The story appeared not long ago in *The Christian Digest* of how George Müller laid hold of the Lord in an hour of crisis. It is told by a captain of a transatlantic vessel who said he could never be the same after having Müller aboard. A heavy fog lay upon the ocean, and the great ship had been brought to a stop. After a while George Müller appeared at the door of the captain's cabin. He knocked and asked for an interview which was granted. "Captain," he said, "I must be in Toronto by Sunday." The Captain, somewhat irritated, gave his intruder to understand that the ship could not move until the heavy fog lifted. "I understand," was Mr. Müller's rejoinder. "But in forty years of service for my Lord I have not failed to keep an appointment. I must be in Toronto Sunday." George Müller asked the captain if he would pray with him. The captain, not a little taken aback, said he would. Together they knelt and Mr. Müller offered a short prayer asking the Lord to lift the fog so the ship might go forward and he might preach Sunday at Toronto. The captain was about to pray, but Mr. Müller stopped him. He said, putting his hand on the captain's shoulder, "You need not pray. You do not believe." As the two walked out on the deck, behold the fog was being lifted. The sun began to shine. In a few moments the ship moved forward. George Müller kept his appointment in Toronto.

Can Christians pray that way? Yes, if they fulfill the conditions, one of which is to believe. Believing is as easy and as natural as breathing when we know God and He possesses us and is given a free rein in our lives. The child who knows a loving parent does not "try" to believe. He rests in a father's love with a certitude which no eventuality can shake. To doubt God is to make Him out a liar as John tells us in his First Epistle. What could be more heinous?

I find it a help to interpret trust in terms of expectation. Someone has said that the answer to prayer is often hindered by the fact that when God's hour strikes and the blessing is sent from the throne, the petitioner is not in a position to receive it in view of the fact that the door of expectation is not open. Some friends once chided George Müller, if I may refer to him again, for saying that his prayers were all answered. His reply was that he had been praying for forty years for two unconverted men, friends of his. He said that he knew that these two would eventually be brought to know the Saviour; for that reason he said that all his prayers were answered. And so it was. Before another year had passed these two men were saved.

The door of expectation must be kept wide open. It is not enough to pray for revival. We must be on the tips of our toes in expectation. Without this there is no true faith. God needs time to work out great things which have to do with the salvation of souls in answer to the prayers of his children. The widow who cried, "Avenge me of my adversary," before the unjust judge, persevered. She held on. She gave the judge no rest. She won because she fully expected to win. The Father in heaven is pleased to see us determined. Our constant expectation moves Him. He is glorified by our faith. Though He tarry long we must not weary. Let us make sure that what we are asking is in keeping with His will and purpose. And then let us be bold as we come to the throne of grace. The answer may come at once. It may be on the way even before we ask as we read in Isaiah, or we may be kept waiting many years. In any case may we not waver. Great is God's faithfulness. He can be trusted with perfect confidence. His promises are sure; they are all yea and amen in Christ Jesus our Lord.

Chapter V

We have come now to one of the deepest of the foundation stones in the structure of prayer. It might be stated in this fashion: To prevail in prayer and to be mighty with God in the fulfillment of His promises, we must be right with our fellowmen. Nothing so affects the Christian's prayer life as his relations with others. Here is where prayer founders; here is where the great short circuit is found through which the prayers of the Church run aground and lose their efficacy.

Jesus our Lord with His customary incisiveness flashes the matter upon the consciences of His followers in this fashion: "When ye stand praying, forgive." He had just said: "What things soever ye desire when ye pray believe that ye receive them, and ye shall have them." But He goes on to say however, it is not as simple as that. Look well to your relations with your fellows. Have you quarrelled with anyone? Go seek your brother and be reconciled. Has someone wronged you? Then you must forgive. Then comes the terrible judgment which might well cause us to tremble: "But if you do not forgive, neither will your Father which is in heaven forgive your trespasses."

It is indeed strange that in books on prayer this matter, in the main, is passed over. Perhaps it is because it is painful. Yet we dare not close our eyes to this aspect of our theme, that is, if we would really learn to pray and release for suffering, despairing mankind the untold riches which God in His great mercy is so eager to bestow. The world's greatest need is for great intercessors that the power and goodness of Almighty God might be brought to bear upon benighted souls as when a great river invades a parched desert land. But great intercessors such as Jacob and Moses and Isaiah and Paul and George Müller and Praying Hyde of India must pay a great price. Nothing costs like prayer. It demands among other things right relations. It costs forgiveness like that wrought on Calvary. I must forgive my brother if I would approach Him who bore all my sins in His body on the Tree that I might be forgiven. In the face of God's forgiveness so freely offered to all men however great their crimes and offenses as regards His love and law, through the Crucified One who was made sin (yea, a curse) that men might be freed from the curse of sin, all petty human bitterness and all unwillingness to forgive become infinite incongruities. Nothing will so get you out of step with God, and so at cross-purposes, as a lack of forgiveness. Though it may hurt like the pulling of all your teeth, you must forgive, or give up the hope of becoming an effective intercessor.

The subject is seen in a little different form in a passage in I Peter which we fail to give its real importance. The scope is simply immeasurable. Peter says that our prayers will be hindered if we fail to give honor "unto the weaker vessel, heirs together of the grace of life"; that is to say, the wife. In other words, how you treat your wife will bear tremendously on your prayer life. If there is wanting the Christian consideration that should mark the way of a Christian husband, it will cut a central nerve in the life of prayer. I live in a land, as a missionary, where wives suffer. It is only in Christian lands where they are given the consideration and the place they merit in God's economy. I was speaking to a group of pastors at a Bible retreat about prayer and asked them if they realized how greatly their prayers would be hindered if they failed to be as considerate of their wives as they should be. They were shocked to learn that the efficacy of their prayers could be impaired by so trivial (in their eyes) a matter. That evening the good wives got together for a little "take-off" on their husbands and sang a song for me, thanking me for the service I had rendered them. You should have seen the looks on the faces of those pastors.

But let us look at the matter in its most significant bearing on prayer. I am praying, let us presume, as I should be praying for revival in the Church. The greatest thing that can possibly take place in this old world with its disease and pain, sin and death, is genuine revival. For real revival means an invasion of the life of heaven as when the ocean sweeps in and bathes the stinking pools of the shores. Pentecost was the life of heaven released upon earth for the healing of its stinking wounds inflicted by sin. But let us presume I pray from a sectarian basis. I am animated by a denominational zeal. I want revival but I want it in my way and for my church. I pray hard and long, but revival does not come. The water of the River of Life clear as crystal which proceeds from the throne and from the Lamb, does not invade my church. It is as dead as ever. Why is my agonized cry not heard? Ah, I am praying with a wrong spirit and from a wrong premise. I must be purged from selfish motives. I must first go to Calvary and die before a resurrection and a Pentecost can be effected. The outpourings of the Spirit in the days of Paul were not simply because of earnest prayers, but the prayers of one who could say: "I am crucified with Christ; nevertheless I live, and yet not I, but Christ liveth in me. . . ."

Missionary labors have taken me to many lands and associated me with almost all the types that make up God's great family today. There is a general conviction that the greatest need is life from heaven, revival, the sort of thing that inflamed hearts and revolutionized lives on Pentecost. Here and there we find life such as that which characterized the Church after Pentecost. False fire, too, of a spurious kind is not wanting. Oh, the longings for genuine revival. And what earnest prayers that God would rend the heavens and come down, that the mountains might melt at His presence, as we read in Isaiah — but the revival does not come. And when one searches into the cause, one is driven to the conclusion that it lies in ourselves. Oh, our divisions, our ill will toward groups of a different ecclesiastical genuflection, our denominational pride, our unwillingness to recognize and aim at the unity of the body with Christ as Head, our zeal for our own particular group with its distinguishing tradition and emphasis, our narrow bigotry, our passionate labors whose end, we say, is Christ but at whose roots there lies the uncrucified flesh. Romans six would, if applied, take care of it all and remove the hindrances as when a prairie fire sweeps the land clear of every vile growth. "Knowing that our old man was crucified together with Christ." Fail to enter into the experience of Romans six and you raise the greatest hindrance to the efficacy of prayer that can be found in the entire brood of obstacles.

I can only pray for revival as I stand on universal ground. I must by faith stand on the oneness of the body of Christ. I must say amen to the prayers of all the saints. I must in spirit embrace all God's children regardless of color. I must be delighted over the growth of some other denomination slightly different from my own — just so souls are brought in true faith to Christ. I must be willing to die, knowing that we who live are always committed unto death for Jesus' sake that the life also of Jesus may be made manifest in our mortal flesh (II Cor. 4:10). My pride and disdain for a brother in the faith whose color makes him obnoxious, will as certainly and effectively close the door of heaven against my prayers as open sin of a heinous nature.

We could almost wish that the Saviour had never said: "If thou bring thy gift to the altar, and there rememberest that thy brother hath ought against thee . . . go thy way; first be reconciled to thy brother." But He said it. It knocks out about one half of the efficacy and worth of the prayers of Christians. If the Church were to really act upon this principle, her prayers could revolutionize the life of nations.

Praying Hyde of India, whose ministry of prayer ushered in a new day, a day of glory and power for the Church of India, tells how on a certain occasion he was giving himself to prayer for certain Indian pastors. He says that he began by saying: "Lord you know how cold and hard, pastor so and so is," when he felt the hand of God sealing his lips. He felt reproved. He began again, but this time it was to thank the Lord for some virtue he was not long in finding his brother had. And so he continued with each one on the list. The result was, as he discovered later, that the Lord poured out a mighty blessing upon each one of these pastors. Ah, the Lord knows our secret thoughts as we read in Psalm 139:4: "For there is not a word in my tongue, but, lo, O Lord, thou knowest it altogether." Indeed, the power of prayer is conditioned upon right relations. The Lord's Prayer (which never was His, but is ours) has no "I" or "me" in it. It is universal ground. As we pray the Lord's Prayer, we embrace all men everywhere, of all colors and conditions and climes. "Forgive us our trespasses, as we forgive." Oh, may it be even so with all who bear the Name of Christ.

Chapter VI

Strange as it may seem, there is today a marked tendency in church circles where faith and power and mighty achievements are the watchword of the hour to attempt to hurdle the law of God's will. We are told that where there is sufficient faith, the sick must be healed. In fact, faith is equated with healing. If healing does not take place, it is because faith has not been strong enough.

What makes this idea so plausible is the fact that Scriptural ground can be found to support it: James 5:15, "The prayer of faith shall save the sick." Nothing could be more true. I have a friend and brother in Christ who was healed of leprosy. Christians of Venezuela know that it is a fact. The marks of the dread disease, though it is as certainly wiped out as in those whom Jesus touched when He walked among men, are still apparent, as palpable as the fact that this dear one is now free from leprosy. It is known far and wide that Jesus the Lord wrought the miracle. These things happen. The Lord Jesus Christ is the same yesterday, today and forever. In His great love and mercy He still responds to the prayer of faith and as of old works wondrous things giving, as the prophet said He would, "beauty for ashes, the garment of praise for heaviness."

But to argue from this fact to which a host of Christians bear witness the world over, that Christ the Lord must heal where there is sufficient faith, is to violate one of the foremost principles of Biblical interpretation. To build a system

35

of doctrine on an isolated text is to concur with the greatest of errors. Truth out of relation with other truths which condition it becomes error. Truth given a proportion which in lieu of other truths it does not merit, leads to fanaticism. To argue from James 5:15 that the Lord must always heal in answer to the prayer of faith is to pass over a host of other texts which when taken into account give a balanced teaching on prayer.

Faith, when it takes a higher position than God's sovereign will, becomes a dangerous entity. Faith, when it rules to one side the purposes of Almighty God, is as much a renegade as the lawlessness and self-will of a criminal. This is no longer faith, but pride masquerading. Faith that sets itself up as a dictator to whom God must bow has more in common with the devils who also believe and tremble, than the Christian who says, "Thy will, not mine, be done."

We have the Saviour's own example: He said that the Son could do nothing of Himself, but only what He saw the Father doing, which He also did likewise. In the supreme crisis of His life, He said: "Not my will, but thine, be done." He was obedient unto death, the death of the Cross.

The case of Paul the Apostle throws great light upon this moot question. He was a sick man and if ever a believer deserved to be healed, it was he. He says he prayed thrice and we can be sure with much fervor. But the answer was "No," though veiled in tender terms as one would expect. "My grace is sufficient for thee." It wrought a mighty transformation in Paul. He said he would, as a result, glory in his weaknesses that the power of Christ might rest upon him. It seems that, in the sublime economy of God, this man, a chosen vessel to bear the Name of His Saviour before kings, must through infirmities of the flesh — a strange malady which he himself called a messenger of Satan to buffet him — be kept altogether broken and helpless in order that the great purposes designed in heaven to be realized through him, might be fulfilled. Only as he depended moment by moment upon Christ His Lord could these purposes be consummated. Any self-sufficiency which physical strength and abounding vitality were almost certain to bring, would be fatal. He must have in himself the answer of death. (See II Cor. 1:8-10.) He must be one who, crucified together with Christ, would say, "I live, yet not I, but Christ liveth in me, and the life which I now live in the flesh I live by the faith of the Son of God, who loved me and gave himself for me."

We have a sound Scriptural basis for this in I John 5:14, 15, "And this is the confidence that we have in him, that, if we ask anything according to his will, he heareth us: And if we know that he hear us, whatsoever we ask, we know that we have the petitions that we desired of him." It is when we ask according to His will *that He hears us*. Once we have His ear and what we ask is in line with His purposes, then we *know* we have the petitions we desired of Him. An absolute certitude comes to us, even before the answer is given, that it will be given.

When we fail to take into account the sovereign will of God, something akin to what happened to Dr. Goodell might befall us. I heard him tell the story some thirty years ago to a group of preachers met together to honor this distinguished pastor. He said that he received a wire from an Anglican bishop requesting him to pray for his son who was sick unto death. He said he gave himself earnestly unto prayer for the son of his ministerial colleague. Some days later another wire came urging yet more earnest prayer for the boy who was so ill. The request was acted upon with great fervor and resolution. Some years later, Dr. Goodell said he met his friend, the bishop, who happened into the city. "Do you recall," inquired the bishop, "my telegrams requesting prayer for my sick boy?" to which the pastor replied that he did. "Well," was the answer, "I fear I did wrong in insisting. It would have been better had the Lord taken my boy at the time. He is grown now, and, oh, what sorrow is mine to see him walking in sin and wickedness." Dr. Goodell closed by saying to the assembly of preachers: "As we pray, it is better to leave the matter with God. He knows what is best."

Now there is firm ground in our praying, and there is ground that is uncertain. I mean to say that there are matters in which we do not need to say, "Thy will be done." We know what God's will is. We know that it is His will that all men should repent of their sins and come to a saving knowledge of Christ. When we pray for the salvation of loved ones, we may and should hold on until the answer comes. Like Jacob we may say: "I will not let thee go except thou [give me my petition]." Scripture affirms that with God nothing is too hard and also that it is not His will that any should be lost. On the other hand, there is ground where we do not know God's will. In the matter of healing, for example, we need to proceed with care. We should and may pray for the sick. And in the main, we know from the Scriptures that the Lord wants His people to be mirrors of health both physically and otherwise. We also know that Christian living means health. But we know that we do not yet have our resurrection bodies and that this mortal frame is destined for death and burial. The Lord often rather than heal the body calls His own home. Or for high and holy ends of a spiritual nature He may permit illness as in the case of Paul.

The story of Eddie Rickenbacker and his companions on their rubber rafts for some twenty-two days out on the Pacific Ocean at the mercy of sun and cold and wind and waves, beautifully illustrates the matter of prayer according to the will of God. It will be remembered that one of the men had a Testament which the group asked him to read to them when they saw the comfort he derived from its perusal. The Word awakened faith and the men began to call on the Lord in their desperate need. The answers came thick and fast. Rain to quench their all-consuming thirst, a bird from the sky to feed their famished bodies, in fact everything they asked for was given. All except one thing: that they might be seen and rescued. This was denied them. They could not understand. Why was it that their Heavenly Father gave them everything they asked for save this the chief desire of their hearts?

Finally one of the men suggested that it must be that it was not God's will that they be sighted. They were in a good school — the school of prayer. They had never before taken into account God's Word or called upon His Name in prayer. Surely the Lord desired for them more training in this wonderful school. Surely, when His purposes were fulfilled and they had had more training in the school of prayer, He would see to it that they would be sighted. And so it was. On the twenty-second day a plane that passed overhead sighted them, and they were rescued. "If we ask anything according to his will, he heareth us."

Chapter VII

In a sense we are wasting our time writing a book on prayer. And those who read are also wasting their time. For we are given to understand in categorical fashion by the authority of the Lord Himself as He speaks through His Word that real prayer lies beyond the ken of man. "We know not what we should pray for as we ought" (Rom. 8:26). The art is so sacred and so high and so holy that man may never hope to enter into its practice except he be taught of the Spirit. The Spirit, we are told, helpeth our infirmities. The Spirit maketh intercession with groanings which cannot be uttered. He maketh intercession for the saints according to the will of God (Rom. 8:27).

So we need not despair. We have a wise and sympathetic and understanding Teacher. It is the Holy Spirit whose temple is the heart of the Christian. He has many functions among which is to be found this. It is his mission to teach the Christian to pray. "He helpeth our infirmities." We do not know how to pray or what to pray for. He points out the objective. He inspires the prayer. We need to wait on the Lord, acknowledging our infirmity, our incapacity. It is then as we wait upon Him in simple faith, that the Spirit takes over. It is then that our praying becomes a cosmic affair, a groaning in the Spirit which cannot be uttered. It is then that we are possessed of a faith which nothing can shake. It is then that mountains are removed and we can laugh at impossibilities.

David Brainerd, the missionary to the American Indians, whose ministry of prayer some historians tell us was the fountainhead of our modern missionary age, discovered as he tells us in his diary, that whenever the Lord purposed to pour out a special blessing upon the Indians, He would first call him aside to wrestle in prayer for it. He had to enter into an agony of prayer. The Lord burdened him; the Spirit drew him with groanings which could not be uttered. He would enter into the sufferings of Christ, filling up, to use one of Paul's expressions, that which was lacking of the Redeemer's afflictions. And then the blessing would come as a veritable tidal wave.

Oh, it is a fearful thing to pray in this fashion. Only God can prepare the believer for such a ministry. The Church waits on such prayer with awe, and well she may, for from such wrestlings hidden from the eyes of men, forged by the Spirit of God on the anvil of the soul's agony, her power (if with God she still has power for the redemption of souls) emanates. Ah, yes, someone must travail in the inspiration of the Holy Spirit if the Church is to go forward.

There are times when the Christian's praying is something so desperate, so awful, so tremendous that one trembles before the very record of it. It is not man's doing; it is God's. It is like the birth throes of a new age. It is an echo of the Saviour's passion. The Holy Spirit alone can carry man's infirmity to such heights. Such a prayer was Moses' when because of Israel's great sin in worshiping the golden calf, he spent another forty days and forty nights on Mount Sinai alone with God whose holy wrath had been so kindled that nothing would satisfy but the destruction of the chosen people. Just what passed between Moses and the Lord, we do not know. But the climax of the prayer is recorded in Exodus 32:31,32. "Oh, this people have sinned a great sin . . . forgive . . . and if not, blot me, I pray thee, out of thy book which thou hast written." How awful, how tremendous, how sublime!

Now it is just not in man to pray with such boldness. The destiny of a nation was in the balance. Moses threw in all he had; yea, his eternal destiny. Nothing mattered but his people. They must be forgiven. It was an echo of the Cross. It was the Spirit of Him who was made a curse that man might be redeemed. Only the Spirit of God can equip feeble man for such a passion and such a position. Little wonder that Moses triumphed. God could not but honor such a faith and crown it with the laurels of victory.

The outstanding example of this kind of praying in our times, though he has been called to his eternal reward, is Praying Hyde of India. One who would learn how to pray and achieve mightily for God and for men must become acquainted with John Hyde. The son of a Presbyterian preacher, he went to India to serve the Lord. As he embarked at New York he found a letter addressed to him in which an elder of the church which his father was serving faced him with a burning question. "John, you are going to India to preach the Gospel. Have you received the fullness of the Spirit or are you trusting in your theological achievements, your learning and your talents?" John was indignant. He threw the letter to one side and went out to pace the deck of the ship as it turned its prow out to the open sea. But the voyage was a long one and John had ample time for reflection. The elder said he would be praying for him. The good man's prayers were heard. John saw his error and turned to the Lord. Many hours were spent in prayer and the study of the Word during the weeks at sea. John sought the Lord for an infilling of the Spirit, and before Bombay was reached a new day had dawned for the fledgling missionary. John made an amazing decision. He resolved that his work in India would be intercession. There were those, of course, who did not understand. John was criticized, but he stuck to his purpose. An overwhelming burden came upon him for the Church in India. The Holy Spirit was upon him and he wrestled with God for a cleansing of the Church and an outpouring of the Spirit that workers in the Lord's vineyard might be empowered. Such was his burden and agony as he groaned in the Spirit that before the great Sialkot convention for thirty days and nights he did not turn down the covers of his bed. He was supernaturally empowered for his holy task — the ministry of prayer. Ah, but what days were those for the Church in India! Missionaries who witnessed the holy scenes still speak with hushed voices of Hyde. The lives of missionaries and pastors and workers were transformed by the hundreds as the Lord rent the heavens in answer to His servant's groanings and wrought miracles in the lives of His followers. Hyde died of a broken heart, but the fruits of his labors were days of heaven upon earth for Christians of India.

The Finney revival that shook the eastern states of America in the first half of the nineteenth century was the fruit of such Spirit-wrought intercession. One whom they called Father Nash would go before the revivalist to the cities he was to visit. Some three or four weeks before the arrival of the evangelist Father Nash would quietly slip into town to prepare the way. With groanings which could not be uttered he prayed in the Spirit for a manifestation of God's glory and power. When Finney appeared to preach the Gospel, a holy awe pervaded the town. There was the presence of God, and the Spirit moved with power convicting souls of sin and "many were the slain of the Lord."

Such praying costs, for as the Spirit takes hold and voices His unutterable yearnings through the Christian's spirit, there's a going down into the Saviour's death and a rising again in the power of His resurrection. II Corinthians 4:11 states that such a participation in the Cross and the empty tomb is indeed a fact. The potency of what may be called "the death — resurrection — mid-process" is released and as a result the graves of many dead in trespasses and sins are opened and the Kingdom of God comes with power.

Some years ago while teaching a Sunday school class of young men, I was greatly shocked one Sunday morning to find a note from a young man whom I considered one of the most faithful members of the class saying he was leaving the class never to return as he considered himself unworthy. It was my first inkling that something was wrong in the young man's life. Naturally I was deeply grieved. What could it be? Some days later I talked to the secretary of the class, an aged missionary lady. She had spoken to the pastor about this lad and had found that the pastor was cognizant of the matter, aware of the nature of the problem, and that he had consulted a physician who said it was best to drop the matter as there was no hope.

One day I spoke to the missionary lady, seasoned by many a prayer battle, asking if we were going to simply take the verdict of medicine as final or call upon God in behalf of this boy we had learned to love. She answered that we should call on God.

"Very well," I said, "then let's pray." We got to our knees in the pastor's study and after a moment or two of prayer we suddenly realized that our prayer was no longer ours. It was in other hands. The Holy Spirit had taken over. We were swept along with a love and passion never before known. Our groanings were the unutterable agonies of the Spirit. We were as spectators looking on. We were borne upon wings as eagles to a climax in which we simply claimed the victory in Jesus' Name. Peace came to our hearts. The next Sunday our boy appeared in class bearing witness that God had broken his chain and that he was now free. Twenty-five years have passed, without a relapse — our boy, now a man, is a faithful member of the church with a radiant testimony for Jesus his Saviour.

Chapter VIII

It is often the case that when prayer does not bring the desired result, praise leads through to victory. There is a power in praise which prayer as such does not have. Of course, the distinction between the two is artificial. Prayer at its best is praise as is evident in the Psalms. "I will bless the Lord," cries the psalmist, "at all times: his praise shall continually be in my mouth" (Ps. 34:1). "Bless the Lord, O my soul: and all that is within me, bless his holy name" — so he charges his soul to fulfill its highest function. "As long as I live," he says, "I will praise the Lord." He calls upon the sun and the moon, all the stars of light, yea, all nature to join him in praising the Lord (Ps. 148). He is resolved that nothing, no personal loss, no catastrophy, no circumstance regardless of its nature shall deter him in this holy practice.

Now let us look into this matter and into the "why" of the power of praise, for prayer can never be the glad and immeasurably fruitful exercise that God intends that it should be unless it is shot through with praise. The reasons are simple enough.

First, praise puts prayer on the highest plane and purges it of unworthy elements. When one comes to God just for things, to ask for this and to ask for that, prayer is cheapened and God is insulted. It cannot be said too often that God is infinitely greater than all His gifts. If I never asked for anything and had Him, I would still have all. There is still a bad taste in my mouth from a book (I was about to say read, but no; I was spared so repulsive an ordeal) I lightly perused by a then famous movie star on prayer entitled *How to Use God.* Though crass and vulgar, it had the virtue of being honest in its egotistical shamelessness. A million times no. Prayer is not the cunning art of using God, subjecting Him to one's selfish ends in an effort to get out of Him what you want. Before prayer can be real prayer in a truly Biblical sense, it must be worship, and that means praise. If God never gave us anything in answer to prayer, and we had Him, we would still be rich beyond measure for time and for eternity; our cup would still be running over and our joy unspeakable. We do not come to God, primarily, to ask for things. We come to worship One who is infinitely adorable, whom to know is to love and whom not even eternity will afford sufficient opportunity to praise. The fact of Calvary alone and the redemption that springs from it, is a blessing so immeasurably great that it sets to ringing all the joy bells of the heart and places one in the position of an indebtedness and gratitude so overwhelming that praise for all eternity is not sufficient.

The saints, using the term in its Biblical sense, all down the ages have realized that when prayer conceived as supplication for certain ends, fails, then praise succeeds. Let us look yet deeper into the reasons. When we offer praise in the face of circumstances quite contrary to our happiness, we take sides with God, who, though He may not have ordered our circumstances by His sovereign will, has, at least, permitted them. The natural bent is to grumble and find fault, and pray from a purely human viewpoint for better conditions. But all things *do* work together for good to them that love God, so nothing is quite so in order as praise. When the dross has been removed from the gold, the refiner will remove the fire. "When thou passest through the waters, I will be with thee . . . when thou walkest through the fire, thou shalt not be burned. . . . For I am the Lord thy God, the Holy One of Israel, thy Saviour" (Isa. 43:2, 3). Job learned the lesson. It would seem as though the furnace was heated seven times more than usual. But Job came forth unscathed. What, unscathed? Nay, transformed, one who could pray for those so-called friends who had so tormented the patriarch with their veiled accusations. It was not when he prayed for himself with all his pestilential sores that he was healed; but it was when he prayed for those who had caused him such mental anguish in the midst of his physical torments, that the Lord turned his affliction. Job had to come completely out of himself. Job died and was resurrected. "Though he slay me yet will I trust him," cried the patriarch. And the end was glory beyond Job's fondest hopes. It was not prayer, as ordinarily conceived, that did the trick. It was something which in its deepest essence was praise. "Though he slay me yet will I trust him" — what a sweet incense before God. This is the language of praise.

The great mystics of the Church all speak of "the dark night of the soul" when the Cross is applied to the last vestiges of the self-life and the soul is liberated from secret self-seeking even in spiritual things and learns to love God for Himself alone. Now this really should be a normal thing in the Christian life. To love God for His gifts is a heinous inversion of values. To love a young lady for the money her wealthy father may have in the bank would be treachery, not love. It cannot be said too often. We must love God not for His gifts but for Himself alone. Somehow for our good and for His praise He must get us to the point of loving *Him*. The process is often a long, painful one. But the stripping must be done. With Paul we must be conformed to the Saviour's death in the power of His resurrection (Phil. 3:10). Let it be clearly understood that there is nothing like praise to carry us through this "dark night of the soul" where Christ the Lord is loved not even for the heaven which He promises, but for Himself alone.

Then, too, nothing has such power to turn our seeming defeats into glorious victories, as praise does. It is when the going is unutterably hard that praise carries us through. We naturally would give way to discouragement and fear and doubt. But the triumph of faith comes when we sing in spite of it all. Paul in prison at Philippi with his back bleeding from many stripes, his feet in the stocks and his cell being the innermost dungeon, sings though it be midnight. The result — an earthquake, prison doors open, the prison keeper himself crying out: "Sirs, what must I do to be saved?" A revival, souls saved, Europe entered into triumphantly with the Gospel, Paul and Silas more than conquerors through Him who loved them — these were the results.

We may not like to admit it but the highest expression of faith is not prayer in its ordinary sense of petition, but prayer in its sublimest expression of praise. Praise, especially when from a purely human viewpoint there is every reason for doubt and despair, is faith in full bloom. The prophet gives us a classical Biblical example in the final words of the closing chapter of the Book of Habakkuk where we read: "Although the fig tree shall not blossom, neither shall fruit be in the vines; the labour of the olive shall fail, and the fields shall yield no meat; the flock shall be cut off from the fold, and there shall be no herd in the stalls: Yet I will rejoice in the Lord, I will joy in the God of my salvation. The Lord God is my strength, and he will make my feet like hinds' feet, and he will make me to walk upon mine high places. To the chief singer on my stringed instruments" (Hab. 3:17-19).

A missionary was passing through a great trial. He had prayed and prayed and prayed, and all to no avail. One day he entered a lonely mission station and found these words in great letters on the front wall: *Have you tried praise?* He was thunderstruck. It was like the voice of God. He had not tried praise. He would do so at once. Getting down on his knees, he offered hearty praise to God for his great trial and arose refreshed. To his amazement he found not long afterward that all was well. His great problem was solved; the trial was over; his joy was unspeakable. Praise had led to victory.

When one looks deeply into the matter one discovers that praise is the most effective means of bringing one in line with the purposes of God. By nature we stand at the opposite pole. We love faultfinding and criticism and murmuring. It is our pride that lies at the roots of our grumbling. Now nothing more effectively than praise divorces us from this fleshly way and swings us over into the life of the new creation in Christ in whom, as we read in Romans six, we died to sin and were made alive unto God. It clinches the matter. The "old man" is an inveterate and utterly incurable grumbler. The new creation in Christ finds the genius of its life in praises to God. It is forever singing and come what may, gives thanks.

A pastor who desired to have a spiritual awakening in his church called the folk together for a week of praise. Each evening they were to meet for but one thing, namely praise. At first it was hard going. The brethren did not understand. It was prayer of the old begging order. Now back of such praying there can be much whining, well masked, of course. The pastor would say: "No, brother, you do not understand. It is praise that I am asking for." By Wednesday a slight change had come. Thursday saw more praises. Friday yet more. By Sunday his folk were in a new frame. A new day had dawned. Sunday was a day such as the church had never seen. It was genuine revival. God's glory filled the temple. Believers returned to their first love. Hearts were melted. The water of life clear as crystal which proceeds from the throne and from the Lamb began to invade the church. It was wonderful. Praise had done it.

"But thou art holy, O thou that inhabitest the praises of Israel" (Ps. 22:3).

CHAPTER IX

THERE IS NOTHING SO DETRIMENTAL TO PRAYER as a wrong motive. Prayer's efficacy is cut down immeasurably the moment the intercessor ceases to seek God's glory. To the degree in which vainglory prevails and "self" looms up as the end, prayer loses its power. There must be the singleness of eye of which our Lord was wont to speak, else He will not be able to release the power of His omnipotence in answer to prayer. The Lord has said that He will not give His glory to another.

This is another way of saying that we are not to seek God for mere personal convenience. Again let it be said that to think of prayer as a means of getting things from God is nothing short of a vulgar degradation of the highest art of which man has any knowledge. We ask and receive not, says James, because we ask amiss. Now we ask amiss when we seek God not for Himself but for things. The Giver is infinitely more than the gift. If we value some blessing for which we pray or some "thing" above God, prayer is degraded and God is dishonored.

The primary office of prayer is communion with God. To have Him is to have all. To lose Him is to lose all. In Him, as Paul puts it in his Epistle to the Ephesians, we are complete. Now to aim at anything less than God Himself is to miss the mark. Unless the Lord in answering our prayers can get us to Himself, He may have to turn to us a deaf ear. The Saviour reproved the multitudes which sought

Him for the loaves and fishes. Then may we never ask for things? Indeed we may. But these things must be sought in and for Him. His Name's honor and glory must be the soul's master passion. It is one thing, for example, for a good wife to seek the Lord for the conversion of, let us say, a husband because it would be so delightful to have him come home not as a drunken sot to beat up the children, but as the neighbor Tom Brown who is a Christian and whose very presence is a blessing to the entire neighborhood. It is another thing for this suffering soul to call upon God for the conversion of her husband so that His Holy Name might be glorified in a life dedicated to the honor and praise of God. If this good wife can say, "Lord bring my husband to know and love Thee that Thy Name might be glorified in him," her prayer takes on an efficacy that heaven cannot resist. The answer will come, for such a prayer God must answer.

"As the hart panteth after the water brooks," cried the psalmist, "so panteth my soul after thee." Here is the right motive. God must be sought for Himself alone. Could aught be compared with Him? Heaven itself would be drab and empty and meaningless without Him. Were He to give us all that we could ask for: Blessings and riches and health and length of days, but not Himself, that were pain and shame and futility and bitter loss too great to fathom. That were hell. If we will but seek first the Kingdom of God and His righteousness we have the promise that all else that is needed will be added to us.

"Our Father which art in heaven, Hallowed be thy name." Here you have it. The prayer opens with the right motive — that God's Name might be glorified. The zeal of His house must eat us up as it did the Saviour. To bring us to that, what purging, what discipline, what tears, what repentance, what an application of the Cross to the old self-life is needed. "Self" dies hard. "They that are Christ's have crucified the flesh." Even so, should one get out of focus with the Cross and fail to let the Holy Spirit apply what has been called "the death — resurrection — mid-process," self will lift its ugly head and lust anew for glory. "Self" is out to rob God of His glory for "the carnal mind is enmity against God: for it is not subject to the law of God, neither indeed can be" (Rom. 8:7, 8).

So we have come back to where we started when we spoke about the law of a right position; that is to say, union with Christ. We have been brought back to the Cross as the basic principle according to which God administers His government. In Revelation five we read that in the midst of the throne there is a "Lamb as it had been slain." In other words, God's throne is now eternally associated with Christ's Cross. Thrones are for government. And Calvary is the basic principle from which God proceeds in His dealings with men. That is why God can be just and yet justify the sinner, and deal with him as a son the moment he believes in the Lord Jesus Christ though he may have trampled underfoot times without number His holy law and mocked and defied Him a million times. Such a man deserves to be cut off forever from God's mercy. Yes, but the Kingdom of God is based on the fact that the chastisement of his peace was upon Christ who bore in His body on the tree the sins of all men.

So much for the divine side which declares that God's dealings with man (repentant, believing man) are mediated through the Cross. Now as to the human, it goes without saying that man's approach to God must also have the Cross as its basic principle. Jesus our Lord is the way; no man cometh unto the Father but by Him. And His way is the way of the Cross. The "old man" as we read in Romans six, was crucified together with Christ. The Christian is simply commanded to reckon himself dead unto sin and alive unto God. Here we have God's method of dealing with that principle which has upset the universe and given Satan such a hold on this old world, the principle which we call sin. It goes without saying that here we have also God's method of dealing with the hindrances in prayer as the Christian approaches the throne of His grace. Pride is the all-comprehensive obstacle. The old "I" can have no dealings with God. Judicially it is a crucified thing. In the midst of the throne is a "Lamb as it had been slain." Now the Lamb is a Man (the God-Man). Man representatively is already in the throne. But to actually get to the throne man must stand where his great forerunner stood: in death and resurrection.

Nothing else can take care of that principle in man which seeks to rob God of His glory. In other words, nothing equips the Christian for prayer like the Cross. It is when he enters by faith and the co-working of the Holy Spirit into the experience of Romans six that he enters into the glories which are the inheritance of those who are single in eye. They have no aim but God's glory, for they have been crucified together with Christ. The motive now is right. In all things they seek but one thing: God's glory. From such a position prayer's power is simply without limit. The Christian now is one with the source of all spiritual riches and power and he may draw on the bank of heaven, as Spurgeon used to put it, to his heart's content. Now as never before, that breath-taking promise of the Saviour, "If ye abide in me and my words abide in you, ye shall ask what ye will and it shall be done unto you," becomes gloriously real.

Here you have the reason, too, why so few Christians enter into the ministry of prayer though urged to do so by the exceeding great and precious promises of God's Holy Word. It costs. "If any man be in Christ, he is a new creature; old things are passed away; behold, all things are become new." It costs the destruction of the "old things."

"Flesh" with its idolatry of "self" and all its corrupt motives must be crucified. The "single eye" which means the scaling of a veritable Everest (nay, Calvary) must be achieved. God's glory must be the goal.

We have a challenging example in that great prayer of Moses which has already been cited. It was on the occasion of Israel's great sin in the worship of the golden calf. Moses said he was afraid of the "anger and hot displeasure, wherewith the Lord was wroth against [Israel] to destroy [her]" (Deut. 9:19). Forty days and forty nights Moses tells us, he fell down before the Lord, as he fell down at the first. It was a long, hard prayer conflict. Moses was determined that the Lord should forgive. "Remember . . . Abraham, Isaac, and Jacob," he cries, "look not unto the stubbornness of this people, nor to their wickedness, nor to their sin." And now we come to the central core of Moses' argument as he pleads his cause. It is a revelation of the basic motive of the great leader's prayer. He was thinking of God's glory. The Lord's great and glorious Name which must be magnified was what had kindled the flames of his passion. Listen to him as he prays: "Lest the land whence thou broughtest us out say, Because the Lord was not able to bring them into the land which he promised them" (Deut. 9:28). Ah, how precious! Moses is concerned about God's glory. The rest is of no consequence. He could not brook the thought of the Egyptians speaking ill of the Lord. He must be glorified in Egypt. Little wonder that he prevails and wins the day.

It is to him whose eye is single that the Lord speaks as in the Song of Songs where the Beloved says: "Thou hast ravished my heart, my sister, my spouse; thou hast ravished my heart with one of thine eyes, with one chain of thy neck." This is something that God cannot resist. It simply overcomes Him. He is led captive. The wealth of His Kingdom is at the disposal of those who seek only

His glory. It is one thing to pray with mixed motives and something vastly different to be actuated by a passion for the glory of God. These are the intercessors whose prayers have changed the course of history and whose cry before the throne of grace has brought a flood tide of blessing upon whole nations. To these heaven can deny nothing. Lord, teach us so to pray.

Chapter X

Much prayer, earnest and fervent as it may be, is of little or no avail not because a faithful Heavenly Father fails to take it into account or is unmindful of His exceeding great and precious promises, but simply because there has been no insight into the situation from which it springs. A right diagnosis has not been made. Matters have not been sized up from God's viewpoint. If we are to pray aright and achieve, we must see things, as it were, with His eyes. God often is moving in one direction and we in another. We have not heeded the divine injunction, "Be still and know that I am God."

To pray the prayer of faith, the prayer of the righteous man which availeth much, we must learn to distinguish the voice of the Lord and know what He is about. Success depends not so much upon our much asking, our persistent speaking, as on our careful listening. "I will stand upon my watch," said the prophet, "and see what he will say unto me . . ." (Hab. 2:1). As we see in chapter one, the prophet had prayed: "O Lord, how long shall I cry, and thou wilt not hear! even cry unto thee of violence, and thou wilt not save! Why dost thou show me iniquity, and cause me to behold grievance? for spoiling and violence are before me: and there are that raise up strife and contention. Therefore the law is slacked, and judgment doth never go forth: for the wicked doth compass about the righteous; therefore wrong judgment proceedeth." How often we cry in similar fashion unto the Lord. There is wrong, there is suffering, there is oppression, we are misunderstood and slanderous tongues sting us as though they were the bite of a serpent; we find ourselves at what has been called "wit's end corner"; we cry unto God but there is no answer. We must do as did the prophet. He decides at last to quiet his soul. He resolves to be still and first get God's viewpoint. The result is miraculous. He does not sit long upon his tower and watch to see what the Lord will say unto him, before the answer comes. "And the Lord answered me and said, Write the vision and make it plain upon tables that he may run that readeth it . . . though it tarry, wait for it, because it will surely come, it will not tarry." All whining ceases and the prophet stands with God in the fulfillment of a terrible judgment upon his people because of pride and idolatry with the Chaldeans as God's instrument. The prophet had been praying his prayer of complaint which was nothing short of a whine and grumble, which got him nowhere. But when he sees things as they really are after a quiet waiting on God, and gets the right diagnosis of the situation, he swings around and prays along the line of God's revealed will and plan and brings to light the fact that Israel is to suffer for corrective purposes which love cannot fail to bring to bear upon her sin, and that the Chaldeans, once the judgment of God is consummated through them, are in turn to be judged for sins even more heinous.

If we would not have our prayers be useless, all weak sentimentality must be consigned to the Cross. We come again to the principle of positional praying. Indeed, it is Romans six where we are told that "the old man" — that corrupt self life — was crucified together with Christ that the body of sin might be destroyed. The carnal mind (see Rom. 8:7) which is enmity toward God and which sees everything in the light of its own interests, judging as good what favors "self," and coldly disregarding the sovereign claims and purposes of God, can never make a right diagnosis of any situation. To see correctly we must stand where Paul stood when he said: "I am crucified with Christ: nevertheless I live; yet not I, but Christ liveth in me: and the life which I now live in the flesh I live by the faith of the Son of God, who loved me, and gave himself for me." The Lord Jesus, our Adorable Saviour, is our example here as in all other matters. He sweat blood in Gethsemane and cried out from the human standpoint, "Father, if it be possible let this cup pass." He could do that for though He was as we read in I Tim. 3:16, God manifest in the flesh, yet it was flesh of our flesh in lieu of which He could be tempted in all points like as we. But this human cry wrung from the Redeemer's soul sorrowful unto death in the hour of the sweat of blood, was followed by another which fully represented God's viewpoint, witnessed to by the wondrous plan of the ages as it appears in Holy Writ, and by the fact that the Lamb of God was in a real sense slain from the foundation of the world, as may be seen in Israel's ancient types. "Not my will, but thine be done." And the Son of God, who was no less the Son of Man, went forth from the dark shadows of Gethsemane to set His face like flint, as the prophet said He would, toward Calvary.

If we could only see what God is aiming at, namely, our conformity as Christians to the image of our crucified Lord, how different our prayer life would be. Paul said that his supreme desire was to be made, in the power of the Saviour's resurrection and the fellowship of His sufferings, conformable unto His death and adds the admonition, on the heels of a passionate expression of his desire to be one with Christ in death and resurrection, "Let us therefore, as many as be perfect, be thus minded" (see Phil. 3:13-15). If we could see the glory of the divine achievement from the viewpoint of heaven and eternity we would not pray for the removal of our particular thorn as did Paul for the removal of his. We would glory in our thorn as also did Paul once he caught a vision of its meaning from the point of view of the throne, and we would give thanks because the Lord is saying, "My grace is sufficient for thee." We would be satisfied knowing that His strength is made perfect in our weakness. Too often we see only from the point of view of time. Our measure is success and health and comfort. God works from the standpoint of eternity with Christian character, into which the Lamb-hood nature of Christ must be worked, as the goal. With conformity to the Crucified as the goal we can glory in that against which and for the removal of which much of our praying has aimed.

We pray that wars might cease and that men might beat their swords into pruning hooks and we have God's Word for it that the day will come when such will eventually be the case. But to expect it *now* would be a violation of sound Biblical interpretation. There is no use praying for millennial blessings *now*. As Christians, of course, we hate the satanic thing called war and may within proper bounds pray for peace. Praise God for all peace-loving souls who pray for understanding among nations. May their number be multiplied a thousandfold. Yet withal, lest we come to despair, let us not overlook the fact that according to the Word of the Matchless One who was not only Priest and King but also Prophet, this present age will close in a time of trouble and a deluge of blood such as history has never known. "Take heed that ye be not deceived. . . . Nation shall rise against nation. . . . there shall be signs . . . upon the earth distress of nations . . . Men's hearts failing them for fear, and for looking after those things which are coming on the earth: for the powers of heaven shall be shaken. And then shall they see the Son of man coming in a cloud with power and great glory. And when these things begin to come to pass, then look up, and lift up your heads; for your redemption draweth nigh" (Luke 21:8, 10, 25-28). The stage is being set. The times of the Gentiles seem to be fast running out. We may and should pray for peace. And God in His great mercy may hold off the judgments (as was the case when Abraham prayed for Sodom whose overthrow was postponed until Lot was delivered), with which, according to Scripture, this wicked age will come to its end. But to expect and to pray for a world order such as Christ's appearing alone can bring, is to proceed on the basis of a wrong diagnosis which is a blind alley that can only lead to despair.

When we pray the prayer with which the Bible closes, the prayer of the seer on the lonely Isle of Patmos, "Come Lord Jesus," we are on safe ground. The Christian revelation of Holy Writ bears witness. We have Christ's Word for it that He is coming again. We have the testimony of the apostles inspired of God. Many of the signs of which the Saviour was wont to speak are even now upon the horizon. Israel is again a nation, as Scripture declares she would be after long centuries of dispersion which the Saviour Himself declared would be the sign of the close of the age of Gentile supremacy. The answer which Christ the Lord gave to John's prayer was, "Surely, I come quickly." Our praying should be along the lines of God's revealed purposes as we look to the future and long for the dawn of a new age, one in which the curse of wickedness, the fruit of a depraved humanity, shall have ended forever. To be governed by weak sentimentality is to bury our heads in the sand as the ostrich does when he sees the storm approaching. The doctrine of the end-time is no popular doctrine. But those who seek smooth sayings and popular doctrines at some point along life's way will have to part company with the One who came to the bitter Cross because His message cut across the grain of human pride like a sharp two-edged sword.

CHAPTER XI

WE HAVE COME TO THE FINAL LAW which seldom is taken into account. It is that prayer must be aimed against God's great foe, the adversary who is forever on the march mobilizing his forces with keen strategy to thwart the Christian's cause and to turn souls against his Christ, the world's Saviour.

This aggressive type of prayer which is nothing short of warfare has abundant Scriptural authorization. In the Old Testament it appears in brutal form in the great type, Israel, ordered to drive out the Canaanites, to destroy their cities, to slay their kings and to annihilate their fortresses. They were to enter into no alliances with these demon-controlled peoples, but were to drive them out mercilessly and in turn possess their land. All this finds a perfect correspondence in the great antitype of the Christian's warfare against the powers of darkness as it is portrayed in the last chapter of Ephesians, where we are told that we wrestle not with flesh and blood but with principalities and powers, the rulers of the darkness of this world, and are admonished to put on the whole armor of God.

Much of the Saviour's ministry and teaching will remain for us an unsolved riddle if we fail to grasp the significance of this great fact of prayer warfare against the powers of darkness. "No man," He said "can enter into a strong man's house and spoil his goods, except he will first bind the strong man; and then he will spoil his house." When the seventy returned from their preaching mission, He said:

"I beheld Satan as lightning fall from heaven. Behold I give unto you power to tread on serpents and scorpions, and over all the power of the enemy: and nothing shall by any means hurt you." The so-called "command of faith" which not only sounds strange to many Christians — and among them Christian workers of no mean category, but only too often is refuted with fiery zeal, was most emphatically laid down as a principle of Christian life and work. In the same breath with which our Lord said, "What things soever ye desire, when ye pray, believe that ye receive them, and ye shall have them," He declared: "Verily I say unto you that whosoever shall say unto this mountain [mountain of satanic oppression] Be thou removed, and be thou cast into the sea; and shall not doubt in his heart, but shall believe that those things which he saith shall come to pass; he shall have whatsoever he saith" (Mark 11:23).

This kind of prayer, no longer in vogue but desperately needed in a world whose ruler is the prince of darkness, and which as never before in all its history is woefully experiencing the agony of satanic oppression (may it not be as we read in Rev. 12 that we are now entering upon that stage of history when the enemy knowing that his time is short has come down with great wrath?), has as its rock-bottom foundation the infinitely significant fact that the Redeemer on Calvary's Cross bruised the serpent's head. No one dare enter upon this warfare who has not been deeply instructed as to the meaning of redemption in its farthermost scope. The Word of God is most concise and unequivocal in its bearing on this matter. Are we not told that through death, the Saviour destroyed him who had the power of death; that its to say, the devil? Are we not given to understand that "having spoiled principalities and powers, he made a shew of them openly, triumphing over them in it [the Cross]"? (Col. 2:15).

But this victory, even as remission of sins or any other blessing that springs from the Redeemer's precious blood shed on Calvary, must be appropriated and made operative through faith. Otherwise the Cross is made of no effect. The enemy and his hosts stalk the land (we are told that he deceives the nations) and takes over even in churches and missions, for where there is worldliness and sin, pride and heresies, rivalries and fleshly ambitions, he finds entrance a simple matter. Where there is no one to challenge his authority on the basis of the Calvary victory he will find a way through subtle machinations in which his uncanny genius is without a parallel, to hold ground and stifle Christian effort. The atmosphere is heavy even in many a church and the Word no longer takes hold with saving power, because the enemy has crept in unawares. The heavens are no longer open for the spiritual manifestation of Him who said, "Lo I am with you alway."

Some Gideon must arise, and girt with the armor of God, must challenge the foe and, releasing the dynamite of the Cross (the word of the Cross is the power — Greek, *dunamis,* from whence comes our word dynamite — of God, I Cor. 1:18), he must strike with sure aim. Panic and destruction in the camp of the enemy will be the result.

There is a most fitting illustration of this in Frazer's *Beyond the Ranges.* It is the story of a pioneer missionary undertaking in villages on the China-Burma border. Frazer says he daily breathed the fumes of hell. He says that the going was so hard that he was about to give up, utterly discouraged, when a tract fell into his hands which focused his attention upon the fact of the Redeemer's victory over the powers of darkness through His death and resurrection. The victory, it was pointed out, had to be appropriated and released in the form of a command of faith. Frazer had never thought of this before nor exercised that kind of faith. Being desperate, however, he decided to try it. He went out into a desert place where he was sure to be alone and unobserved and then gave the command of faith hurling, as it were, the fact of the victory of Calvary into the enemy's ranks. He praised God at the top of his lungs for the Saviour's victory and in His Holy Name commanded the enemy and his hosts to flee. Frazer says it was the turning point in his desperate fight with paganism. The tide turned. The missionary tells how later a mighty revival swept through these villages on the border of Burma effecting marvelous transformations, God's Kingdom being established where formerly Satan reigned.

Victory is not always that dramatic. It may be wrought silently on one's knees. Quietly the Christian may take a stand in his home where, let us presume, the peace of God which passeth all understanding has not prevailed. There have been tensions, impatience, harsh words, criticism, a heavy atmosphere has robbed the home of its joy. The enemy is forever seeking to inflame the "self-life" with its touchiness and fussiness, its murmurings and its jealousies. The Cross must be brought to bear on this situation. First, as we read in Galatians five where "the works of the flesh" are so mercilessly delineated with the categorical verdict, they that are Christ's have crucified the flesh with its affections and lusts. Second, a "stand" must be taken against the working of evil spirits who are out to wreck so far as is possible the Christian home. "Your adversary the devil, as a roaring lion, walketh about, seeking whom he may devour: Whom resist steadfast in the faith . . ." (I Pet. 5:8, 9). Jesus the Lord was manifest to destroy the works of the devil. So we are on solid Scriptural ground when in His Name we claim their destruction.

Or it may be a Christian mission far out in pagan lands where through jealousies and pride and envy and personal ambition, the enemy has gained ground on which to stand. The atmosphere is heavy and the Spirit of God is no longer moving with power, giving liberty and joy. Ordinary prayer of the begging type brings no relief. What is to be done? The enemy must be "bound" and cast out. This may not be achieved overnight. The fight may be long and hard. But the victory of Calvary if persistently held up in faith against the evil one and his agents cannot but eventuate in an overthrow of the enemy's strongholds and a glorious clearing in the spiritual atmosphere; one in which the Holy Spirit will manifest Himself to work great things.

Or it may be a seminary in which the great essentials of the Christian faith are being denied and the vain and futile philosophies of men are made to take their place. One may fight with carnal weapons to no avail. Things may even get worse. However, when some good soldier of Christ who finds himself involved, recognizes at the back of it all the subtle working of Satan and his agents and takes a stand against the powers of darkness, claiming the destruction of their works in the Name of Him who put an end to the rule of the prince of darkness on Calvary, and fights it out, as it were, in the heavenlies with weapons which are not carnal but mighty through God, there comes at last a visible crumbling on the purely human and material side. The victory once won in the unseen realms where the powers of darkness held sway, the edifice of heresy soon goes to pieces on the physical level.

It would seem as though the Christian today is becoming increasingly aware of a purely spiritual and unseen force which the Bible calls the powers of darkness, determined to disturb him through accusations, and relentless in their efforts to stir up fears and doubts. The Christian's only recourse is prayer. "Lord," cried the psalmist, "preserve me from the fear of the enemy." In Psalm 149 we are told of "the judgment written" which all the saints are to execute.

"Now is the judgment of this world," said Jesus our Lord, as he entered upon *La Via Dolorosa* which led to the Cross; "Now is the prince of this world cast out." "Now is come salvation, and strength, and the kingdom of our God, and the power of his Christ: for the accuser of our brethren is cast down, which accused them before our God day and night. And they overcame him [the dragon] by the blood of the Lamb, and by the word of their testimony; and they loved not their lives unto the death. Therefore rejoice, ye heavens, and ye that dwell in them" (Rev. 12:10-12).

Chapter XII

It follows from the fact that when we pray God works, that prayer can become a nation-shaking, history-making, world-moving affair. "Call unto me and I will answer thee, and will show thee great and mighty things, which thou knowest not." It is not that prayer as such is so mighty, but God is, who promises to work great and mighty things if His children will but pray. The Living God with whom nothing is impossible, for He is the Almighty, can change the course of history, transform the life of a nation, and cause wars to cease in answer to prayer. The pages of Holy Writ where we have the story of God's chosen people and the coming of the Holy One, the promised Messiah, the world's Redeemer, with the birth of the Church and its world-embracing movement of redemption, give abundant evidence of this fact. The history of Christian missions abounds with examples. So-called profane history is not wanting in proofs of the power of prayer. Let us consider just a few such cases.

When Moses prayed for forty days in the holy mount to which he returned after Israel's heinous sin in the worship of the golden calf, we read that the Lord said to him: "Let me alone that I may destroy them." Moses was afraid of the anger and hot displeasure of the Lord (Deut. 9:19), but he did not let Him alone. By no means. He fought one of the mightiest prayer battles of all time. The great law-giver might have relinquished and rested in a self-complacent consciousness of a future glory somewhat personal, for the Lord said: "I will make of thee a nation mightier and greater than they." But he was undaunted. His prayer comes to a majestic climax (one that brings to mind the majesty of the One who prayed that His murderers might be forgiven) in the words: "Oh, this people have sinned a great sin, and have made them gods of gold. Yet now, if thou wilt forgive their sin —; and if not, blot me, I pray thee, out of thy book which thou hast written" (Ex. 32:31, 32). Little wonder that Moses triumphs. Furthermore, there is added weight and power to Moses' prayer in the fact that his chief concern was God's glory. His plea is for forgiveness, "Lest the land whence thou broughtest us out say, Because the Lord was not able to bring them into the land which he promised them" (Deut. 9:28). A mighty victory in prayer was the result, a victory the like of which is not to be found in the pages of the Old Testament which teem with great prayers, and so the destiny of a nation was determined. How true is the saying that our prayers are worth what we are worth. Moses threw in everything that he had even to his own eternal happiness and stood in the breach for Israel. Such prayers cannot be gainsaid even when the future of a nation is at stake.

We have David's great prayer at the time of Absalom's revolt when the king had to flee in shame. The cause of the great king seemed lost as the usurper marched triumphant into Jerusalem, Israel's capital, and sat upon the throne of David. But the king was a man of prayer as witness the Psalms. We have the story of David's anguish and prayer in the third Psalm: "Lord how are they increased that trouble me! . . . Many there be which say of my soul, There is no help for him in God. . . . But thou, O Lord, art a shield for me; my glory, and the lifter up of mine head. I cried unto the Lord with my voice, and he heard me out of his holy hill. . . . I laid me down and slept; I awaked; for the Lord sustained me. I will not be afraid of ten thousands of people, that have set themselves against me round about. . . . Salvation belongeth unto the Lord: thy blessing is upon thy people. Selah." The victory which later was won on the field of battle and the tragic end of Absalom and the consequent re-establishment of King David upon his throne, was first won in the unseen realm of prayer when to Messiah's great type the assurance was given that his cry had been heard. Indeed, the destiny of kings and of nations may be determined by the knee that bows in the presence of God, and in the voice of supplication that reaches the throne of grace.

Read the Book of Daniel and see how his prayers shook first the great Babylonian Empire and then the Medo-Persian. He feared not the decree of the king and refused to worship the image that had been set up. He defied wicked political connivers who sought to undo him. "Now when Daniel knew that the writing was signed, he went into his house; and his windows being open in his chamber toward Jerusalem, he kneeled upon his knees three times a day, and prayed, and gave thanks before his God, as he did aforetime." Such defiance of the king's decree, for the plotters who had been watching immediately took word to his majesty, brought down upon the prophet the punishment stipulated by the king's decree, being cast as he was into the den of the lions. I need not go into details over the glorious victory of the prophet. Who does not know of the angel who stopped the mouths of the lions, and of the terrible end of the wicked politicians who had sought Daniel's life? My point is that the king's decree resulting from the deliverance that God had wrought must have shaken the empire to its very foundations. "Then king Darius wrote unto all people, nations, and languages, that dwell in all the earth; Peace be multiplied unto you. I make a decree,

That in every dominion of my kingdom men tremble and fear before the God of Daniel: for he is the living God, and stedfast for ever, and his kingdom that which shall not be destroyed, and his dominion shall be even unto the end. He delivereth and rescueth, and he worketh signs and wonders in heaven and in earth, who hath delivered Daniel from the power of the lions."

Paul's midnight prayer in that innermost cell of the prison at Philippi made history. It was one of the most decisive moments in the history of mankind, for this man, God's chosen vessel, was Christianity's foremost herald of the Cross. Would he enter Europe with the glad tidings of the Gospel of Christ, according to the call of the man of Macedonia who in a vision had said to the apostle: "Come over and help us"? The powers of darkness had said no! Scourgings and the stocks and a dank prison cell were their answer. "And at midnight Paul and Silas prayed and sang praises unto God." Ah, that settled the matter. Paul *would* enter triumphantly into Europe to proclaim the message of the Cross. The foundations of the prison were shaken. The prison keeper cried out: "Sirs, what must I do to be saved?" The glad tidings of a Saviour's love were proclaimed and the voice of this the chief maker of history who laid the foundation of a Christian order in the great centers of the Roman Empire, was heard in the strategic cities of Greece and later of Europe. Is it not written: "Call unto me in the day of trouble and I will deliver thee and thou shalt glorify me"?

The greatest prayer of all the years of mankind's travail was the Son of Man's cry of agony in the garden. Here it was that the eternal destiny not only of nations but of the entire race was determined. For in that bitter cry, "Father, if it be possible let this cup pass," was the possibility, humanly speaking, of the abyss swallowing up the children of men in an eternal night of woe, for the Saviour held in

His hand the key. He must go to the Cross; He must climb the hill of Calvary. He who knew no sin must be made sin for us that we might be made the righteousness of God in Him. No, it was not the fear of death — death as martyrs are wont to meet it. It was the awful curse of the sin of the world which He must bear. Little wonder the sweat of blood, the awful cry of anguish, and the unrequited quest for a bit of comfort in the companionship of the apostles who slept. But the Son of Man comes forth triumphant. The battle is won. The sinful race with its pain and its shame and its death shall find deliverance — yea, shall find heaven itself in the remission of sin and an all-inclusive redemption in the blood of the Redeemer's Cross. What is written of Him shall be fulfilled. It was in prayer that our Lord achieved the victory which only a few hours later was sealed on Calvary. For the essence of that awful prayer, the most significant of all the ages was not, "if it be possible let this cup pass," but "nevertheless, not my will but thine be done."

But it is not only in the pages of Holy Writ that we find prayers which determined the course of history. Let us turn now to the history of the Church. We choose one case from the abounding myriads. A more critical hour in the life of the Church could not be found than when Count von Zinzendorf began to call upon the Lord in 1714 in Herrnhut, Germany. He was bowed down in an agony of soul because of what he saw among Protestant believers of the different evangelical movements. It was a time of fiery persecution. Luther had done his work. Calvin had wrought in a mighty way. Huss was a sacred memory. Zwingli had led his followers. But there was confusion and the blood of Protestant martyrs continued to flow. Count von Zinzendorf was a man of affairs and an ardent Christian from boyhood. He decided to open the doors of his great estate to persecuted evangelicals of Europe that they might find a refuge from the storm. Christians came from far and near — believers of every theological color and of all the sects.

Then began Zinzendorf's travail. He had hoped for love and understanding. What he heard was the voice of controversy. Strife over a thousand and one secondary matters in the realm of doctrine and practice was bitter and unceasing. Zinzendorf longed to see God's people one even as the Saviour had prayed, and on fire with a holy zeal for missions. As to foreign missions, Protestantism was dead. Her life was being consumed in endless theological strife. Oh, to see the wounds of Christ's body healed and to see it function in fulfillment of the Church's marching orders: "Go ye into all the world and preach the gospel." Von Zinzendorf spent whole nights in prayer. Others caught the spirit and joined him, filling up what was lacking of the afflictions of Christ.

The answer came on August 14, of the year 1714. Zinzendorf called for a communion service which all might attend. It was in the partaking of the emblems of the Saviour's broken body that "the Sun of Righteousness arose with healing in his wings." The glory was more than flesh could bear. Believers were prostrate in the presence of God. The Cross in all its vast significance was unveiled. When the congregation arose an immeasurable transformation had been wrought. Henceforth Christ was all and in all. The so-called Moravian movement got under way. They prayed with the clock, groups taking their turns, twenty-four hours of the day for ten years. The result? In twenty-five years one hundred missionaries had gone forth to all parts of the globe. These Moravians spearheaded a world-wide movement in the preaching of the Gospel which eventually swung Protestantism from polemics to missions. The great century of modern missions owes all to von Zinzendorf and the Moravians. John Wesley, himself a spiritual child of the Moravians, after the great experience of Aldersgate, went to Herrnhut to observe firsthand what the Lord was doing. He wrote home to friends, saying: "I have found a church in which one breathes the very atmosphere of heaven." If ever prayers made history, those of Count von Zinzendorf did. Witness modern missions.

Profane history is not wanting in examples of prayer as the determining factor in the great crises that are wont to develop in the course of events, national and international. Dunkirk stands for the darkest hour for the Allies in World War II. France had fallen and three hundred thousand British soldiers were fleeing toward the channel. Hitler laughed insolently. Yes, the backbone of the British army would soon be annihilated. There was no hope for Tommy, humanly speaking.

It was then that King George VI decreed a day of prayer throughout the British Empire. Many of us who are not under the Crown took part. Ah, what a day, for God rent the heavens and came down. He laid bare His holy arm and wrought as He alone can. On the side of the German forces came a storm such as had never been witnessed. Every plane was grounded. Tanks were bogged down in mud. In the grip of the storm not a soldier moved. On the British side the channel was like glass. Never was the water quieter. Thousands of boats plied all day long across the channel — even women in small craft came to the rescue. Two hundred and ninety thousand British soldiers were saved. The island was never invaded. Hitler was stopped at Dunkirk. How? God intervened in answer to prayer, for if ever there was a just cause in the many conflicts which have drenched the earth with blood, which the Lord who governs the universe could righteously favor, it was that of the Allies in World War II. The British soldiers, according to an article which appeared in the official organ of the

Officers' Christian Union, an army organization, seeing the Hand of God working their deliverance, formed circles of prayer to give thanks. It is still written: ". . . call upon me in the day of trouble: I will deliver thee, and thou shalt glorify me" (Ps. 50:15).

Lord, teach us to pray.

Chapter XIII

GOOD REASONS

IT WOULD APPEAR STRANGE that the Lord should be moved by a good argument. One smiles at the thought of the Most High being influenced by sound reasoning; yet such is the case. We have God's own Word for it that, if I may so speak, He likes a good argument. In Isaiah 41:21 we read: "Produce your cause, saith the Lord; bring forth your strong reasons." In other words, "Come, argue the case with me; why do you ask for this?"

We should not be shocked by such a statement. When we give it thought, we see that this is altogether in keeping with the divine order. God made us after His own image; that is to say, rational beings. Only reasonable procedures can please the Lord. We have greatly erred in thinking that we must find firm foundations for our prayers in emotion. Tears, of course, are in order, for the Saviour Himself, as we read in Hebrews 5:7, offered up prayers and supplications with strong crying and tears and was heard. Emotion has its place, but the stories in Holy Writ of the prayers of the prophets and apostles and great men of God point rather to the fact that we must find in sound reasoning the secure ground, the unshakeable foundation necessary in order to stand before the Lord and prevail in prayer.

Needless to say, and this is in a sense repetition, but it bears repetition as nothing in all the universe, the soundest argument that could ever be found by an intercessor seeking the ear of God, lies in the holy Name of

Jesus. If we ground our prayers in the Saviour's Cross where union between God and man was effected, we have the strongest reason that it is possible for a sinful man to bring before his Heavenly Father. "Whatsoever ye shall ask the Father in my name, he will give it you. Hitherto have ye asked nothing in my name: ask, and ye shall receive, that your joy may be full" (John 16:23, 24). It is the Name of Jesus, the Name which is above every name, which opens the door. When I plead the atoning death of my Redeemer who bore my sins in His body on the tree, I have no difficulty in reaching the ear of God; yea, I know for a certainty that I shall not be denied an audience with my King. "Bring forth your strong reasons, saith the King" (Isa. 41:21). You will never find a stronger reason than the Name of Christ.

From here we descend to lesser arguments, and their name is legion. The intercessors of the Scriptures appealed to reasons of one kind or another, all of a valid nature and of great weight, to reinforce the efficacy and power of their supplications as they brought their petitions before the Lord. When Moses prayed for Israel on the occasion of her great sin in the worship of the golden calf, pleading for forgiveness he cried: "Remember thy servants Abraham, Isaac and Jacob." When Samson prayed for strength in the temple of the Philistines, having been shorn of his might because of his folly, he said, "O Lord God, remember me, I pray thee, and strengthen me, I pray thee, only this once, O God, that I may be at once avenged of the Philistines for my two eyes," and his prayer was heard. When Hezekiah prayed for deliverance at the time of Sennacherib, King of Assyria's invasion, when it seemed that Jerusalem would surely fall, he pointed to the blasphemy of the king's general and said: "Now therefore, O Lord our God, save us from his hand, that all the kingdoms of the earth may know that thou art the Lord." Hezekiah stood on solid ground; he produced his cause, bringing forth strong reasons, and was heard. A great deliverance ensued. We read, "And the Lord sent an angel, which cut off all the mighty men of valour, and the leaders and captains of the camp of the king of Assyria."

When Daniel set his face unto the Lord God as he himself tells us (Dan. 9:3) "to seek by prayer and supplications, with fasting, and sackcloth, and ashes" deliverance for his people who were bearing the rigors of a divine judgment in Babylonian captivity because of their idolatry and sin, it was on the basis of a promise which he had discovered in the Book of Jeremiah, according to which the Lord would accomplish seventy years in the desolations of Jerusalem. The time was about up. Daniel, as he broods over the promise, is stirred to the very depths of his soul by a great hope for his suffering people. He girds his mind, humbles himself and lays hold of the Lord his God, confessing the sins of his people. "O Lord," he prays, "I beseech thee let thine anger and thy fury be turned away from thy city Jerusalem, thy holy mountain." Ah, what a burden was his when he contemplated the shame, the desolation, yea, the curse that had been poured upon his people, chosen of God as they had been for the realization of the Messianic hope! From a purely human viewpoint no star was to be found in the night of Israel's shame. But the prophet had found a clear-cut promise which the Lord had made to Jeremiah that at the end of seventy years of reproach and chastisement, Israel should be restored. That was sufficient. The Lord could not fail to keep His Word. Here was a strong reason. Here was unshakeable ground from which to pray. Armed with the promise, Daniel prayed through to victory. An angel was sent to comfort him. Israel was restored. Messiah the Prince came. His work was consummated on Calvary's Cross. Daniel was given to see it all in a vision, how the Messiah should be cut off, "but not for himself," as we read in Daniel 9:26.

We were saying that the Lord bids us bring forth strong reasons as we come before Him in prayer. Our cause must be well grounded. Can we produce a good argument, present a sound reason worthy of the consideration of One so High and so Holy? For God to act, there must be claims brought to bear upon His righteous government, based as it is upon a moral order so lofty as to be beyond the ken of man, claims of such a nature as to merit the intervention of the Father of Lights. Such a claim is a promise which He Himself has made. What assurance is given, what confidence is awakened when we find in Holy Writ a promise that fits our need. Psalm 50:15 covers the whole gamut of human suffering. We are simply told to call unto the Lord in the day of trouble, with the promise that He will deliver. Our prayer takes on an efficacy that cannot be gainsaid when we accept the condition with which the promise is made and say, "By Thy grace, I promise henceforth to glorify Thee."

The Bible, we have said, has been called a textbook on prayer. Here are the laws of prayer and here are mighty men of God achieving ends of immeasurable significance through prayer. As we study these great prayers of the Scriptures, we discover that they all obey this simple law which we call "the law of a good argument or a strong reason." If we can only get our feet on ground that is solid in this respect, the battle is more than half won.

We know from the gospels where we read of our Lord healing the sick, cleansing the lepers, opening the eyes of the blind and raising the dead, that the exposure of man's need and pain before the eyes of the Most High, and a simple cry for help are of vast significance. Such a cry never went unheeded. Man's pain and need, when pressed upon the One who governs the universe and who, as we

see in the face of Jesus Christ, is infinitely good and merci-
ful beyond measure, are bound to have a glorious effect.
Yet pain often goes unalleviated in the face of earnest
prayer for help because, as we see in Paul's unanswered
prayer (answered in a higher way than he had thought),
the highest ends of a loving Heavenly Father for man are
only attained through discipline and trial.

If to our plea for help in the midst of life's vicissitudes,
we bring to bear the higher claims of God, namely, that
His Name may be glorified, we of course move onto ground
which cannot be shaken. Then we become invincible. And
if to this we find a way to harness our puny plea for help to
the great purposes of God in the proclamation of the Gospel
and the furtherance of Christ's Kingdom, then we begin
to pray with the spirit and vigor of a Paul or a David
Brainerd or a George Müller, or a Praying Hyde, and we
must be heard and great things will be wrought. "And
when they [the apostles] had prayed, the place was shaken
where they were assembled together; and they were all
filled with the Holy Ghost, and they spake the word of God
with boldness" (Acts 4:31).

Chapter XIV

It is indeed a breath-taking affirmation which our Lord makes in Matthew 18:19, "If two of you shall agree on earth as touching any thing that they shall ask, it shall be done for them of my Father which is in heaven." There is just no limit, says the Saviour, in effect, to the power of this kind of prayer. The question naturally arises, "Why?" The answer leads us deep into the mystery of the Church in union with her divine Head, and the union which in the thought of God should prevail among those who form the body of Christ, which is the Church.

The sort of agreement which our Lord has in mind is something which no human agency can bring about. It goes deeper than the ties of race or caste or family or any other bond between hearts. It is the fruit of a common union with Christ. Between two who own Him as Lord and who are possessed of His Spirit, there is a oneness which the Saviour likens to the oneness which is His with the Father (see John 17:23). Where such a fusion of spirits takes place, Christ Himself is present as He affirms in the following verse (Matt. 18:20), "For where two or three are gathered together in my name, there am I in the midst of them."

Now it follows as an inevitable consequence that where such a chain exists, where two are one by His Spirit with the Lord Jesus Himself as the reigning Sovereign, Head of the Church, a wrong kind of praying including purely human aspirations of a more or less selfish nature, is simply not possible. A union such as that mentioned in the Scriptures can only exist where God is supreme as the unseen link, unseen but real as nothing else in all the universe is real, and where all lesser motives are lost sight of in an all-consuming desire that He might be glorified. It stands to reason that prayer from such a foundation and such a spring must have a scope and power that cannot be measured. It is even as our Lord affirms and nothing less: "If two of you shall agree on earth as touching any thing that they shall ask, it shall be done for them of my Father which is in heaven."

One alone, however great his spiritual stature, cannot do this kind of praying nor achieve such results. That it may be the body, the entire Church represented, it must be at least two. Naturally, there is a crescendo, an ever-enhancing power, as the number increases. But as the number increases and the power, so do the difficulties in obtaining such a oneness as the Saviour postulates. Oh, if the Church could realize what lies within her grasp for the redemption of souls and the establishment of the Kingdom of God, in the realm of corporate intercession, surely she would be willing, as we read in Galatians 5:24, to "crucify the flesh" with its warring aims and its factional goals, and so stand in that oneness which is so quickly brought about when the Holy Spirit is in control and has full sway.

The classic Biblical illustration of the power of prayer as it emanates from such a spring is found in Acts twelve, where we have the story of Peter's imprisonment in Jerusalem. King Herod had killed James, the brother of John, with the sword and had proceeded further to take Peter also. What an hour for the struggling infant Church surrounded by such relentless forces bent on her destruction. The words of Scripture are graphic: "Peter therefore was kept in prison, but prayer was made without ceasing of the church unto God for him." Little wonder that such a mighty miracle (and I use the term advisedly) was wrought. I shall quote the entire passage as it is in Acts 12:7-10:

> And behold, the angel of the Lord came upon him, and a light shined in the prison: and he smote Peter on the side, and raised him up, saying, Arise up quickly. And his chains fell off from his hands. And the angel said unto him, Gird thyself and bind on thy sandals. And so he did. And he saith unto him, Cast thy garment about thee, and follow me. And he went out. . . . When they were past the first and the second ward, they came unto the iron gate that leadeth unto the city . . . and they went out, and passed on through one street; and forthwith the angel departed from him.

The kind of praying that brought these results, human nature being what it is, is well-nigh impossible to attain. The "flesh" is strong, and as we read in Galatians five, its works are divisions, hatred, variance and strife. Yet when the Cross is applied to the citadel of the heart where secret pride is enthroned and a thorough crucifixion of the "self-life" is wrought, such a union of spirits comes about in a natural way, and prayer of this invincible order becomes a stupendous reality.

I have just witnessed it in Colombia where Christians are going through the fires of persecution, homes and temples are being burned and believers are being put to the sword. Such an experience fuses spirits into one. It was so in Jerusalem when the Church prayed without ceasing for Peter in chains awaiting execution.

During the celebration of the first centenary of the coming of the Gospel to Colombia, great gatherings were planned to be held in the leading cities. The Church with her different denominations, independent groups, and missions of one "persuasion" and another, *moved as one*. It was wonderful beyond words! It was like a great orchestra with its leader, in perfect harmony under one will. The results were exactly what the Saviour says about prayer when

Christians are one in the Holy Spirit. Prayers were answered in such an overwhelming fashion that the days passed as a never-ending chain of victories. Only at one place was there a stoning, and that without real harm to anyone's person. God wrought the impossible. The great celebrations with evangelistic campaigns, united choirs singing the praises of the Lord and Bible retreats, were held without a serious mishap, all in a spirit of victory and joy unspeakable.

Some years ago a fellow missionary and I labored among the soldiers of the land of my adoption, preaching the Gospel. This went on for five years in and out of camps and up and down the highways of the nation, which in those days were guarded by soldiers. The experience in prayer was, so to speak, worth a million. My fellow missionary and I were so perfectly one in spirit that we had only to ask the Lord, and it was given. We lived in a world of miracles like those of the Book of Acts. Nothing daunted us. We had only to ask, I repeat, and it was given. The difficulties from the natural, human angle were of no significance. Had not the Saviour said, "If two of you shall agree on earth as touching any thing that they shall ask, it shall be done for them of my Father which is in heaven"? He had said it, and that was sufficient. And as we prayed and believed, we found the promise to be true.

Discouraged prayer warrior, find a prayer companion with whom you can be perfectly natural, one with whom you can stand in a perfect spirit of oneness in a common Saviour, and enter with this one upon a glorious adventure of prayer. If you cannot find such a prayer partner, ask the Lord to raise him up for you. It shall be done. A new day will dawn of such a glory and beauty as you never dreamed was possible this side of heaven.

"And at midnight Paul and Silas prayed." Do you wonder that an earthquake shook the prison where they lay bound? Does it seem strange that this same night Paul and Silas, freed from the stocks, were able to lead the prison keeper to a knowledge of Christ? Not when we consider the Saviour's word, "Again I say unto you, That if two of you shall agree on earth as touching any thing that they shall ask, it shall be done for them of my Father which is in heaven."

The missionary stands in a peculiar position with never-ending opportunities to prove the power of prayer. Some years ago in this land to which my heart is now bound by ties which are only forged in the propagation of the cause of Christ, Communism came in as a flood which threatened to overthrow the old order and take over the country. Education was revamped on a basis of atheism; night after night from radio stations blasphemy was poured out over the land; a terrific tension gripped hearts, and fear with paralyzing power took over. A group of pastors and missionaries came together to see what could be done. The conclusion was that the only hope was divine intervention. Had not the Lord said, "Call unto me in the day of trouble and I will deliver thee"? The decision was to meet each morning at six-thirty for prayer, and to hold on until deliverance came.

Weeks went by and then months while they held firm in prayer. Never a morning did the prayer warriors fail. They found themselves in a mighty conflict with the powers of darkness. They wrestled not with flesh and blood but with principalities and powers. They represented different denominations, but all thought of sectarianism was lost. In the awful crisis of the hour they became absolutely one in Christ. One great passion consumed them. For six months in the early morning hours they bombarded heaven with strong crying and tears. These were not formal gatherings for prayer. Pastors and missionaries were down on their faces before God pleading the promise and claiming the victory in Jesus' name.

And then one glad morning after six months of groaning in the Spirit before the throne of grace, one of the pastors came in with the morning paper. There was the answer. The president had dismissed the "Reds" from the cabinet and had turned rightabout-face. The dark cloud that had been upon the nation lifted. The Sun of Righteousness appeared with healing in His wings. The backbone of the monster was broken. God had laid bare His mighty arm and had wrought a glorious deliverance. Fear was gone. Joy flowed like a river which swept everything before it. There was gladness like in the days of Queen Esther. As I listened not long after to a local radio staion, I was moved beyond measure. "Lord Jesus, I love thee, asleep in the hay," was the song. Years have gone by, and there is no sign of the monster's return to power. Oh, yes, if we will only agree according to the Saviour's promise, there is no limit to the power of prayer.

Chapter XV

At first it would appear altogether out of order, if not contrary to reason, to close this series of meditations on prayer by sounding a negative note. After the victorious affirmations of the foregoing chapters regarding the power of prayer and the absolute assurance based on the Word of God that the ear of the Almighty, whose loving care is ever about His children, never fails to heed their cry, however faint, why now in closing raise this question? Why now open the door to doubts which we have sought by every means to banish? The answer is, we must be honest. We must be true interpreters of the Word. We must be true to experience. Who that is a follower of the Lord Jesus Christ has not experienced the pain, yea, the agony of an unanswered prayer? As the pages of Holy Writ abound with examples of answered prayer, so do they also give us abundant proof of unanswered prayer. And as we look with reverent devotion into these Biblical examples of defeat, and take into account the plain teaching of the Word as to the *why* of the unanswered prayer, we find that this seemingly negative side of the matter is fraught with vast meaning and is virtually a mine where gold such as that only found in the treasures of God, is at the disposal of the Christian. He must have this negative emphasis to bring to yet sharper focus the positive.

As we enter upon the *why* of the unanswered prayer, we are compelled to head the list with a most unsavory thing, which like the poor to whom the Saviour referred, is ever with us in one form or another. Yes, it is that heinous thing the Bible calls sin, and which the world is so eager to dress up and call by some other name. Sin strikes at the foundations of prayer, and vast as its power is, renders it ineffective. How often we come upon such words as these as we leaf over the pages of Holy Writ, "Your sin has come between you and me; because of your sin I will not hear you." It comes to perhaps its severest intonation in Proverbs where the Lord quite frankly says:

> Because I have called and ye refused; I have stretched out my hand, and no man regarded; But ye have set at nought all my counsel, and would none of my reproof: I also will laugh at your calamity. . . . Then shall they call upon me, but I will not answer; they shall seek me early, but they shall not find me . . . They would none of my counsel: they despised all my reproof. Therefore shall they eat of the fruit of their own way, and be filled with their own devices. For the turning away of the simple shall slay them. and the prosperity of fools shall destroy them (Prov. 1:24-32).

The psalmist understood this and was saying "amen" in hearty fashion, when he said, "If I regard iniquity in my heart, the Lord will not hear me: But verily God hath heard me; he hath attended to the voice of my prayer. Blessed be God, which hath not turned away my prayer, nor his mercy from me" (Ps. 66:18-20).

Perhaps the most poignant example in all the Scriptures is that of David when he lay on the cold ground all night pleading for his sick baby. But the baby died. David's prayer was not heard, for David had committed an abominable sin. His hands were red with the blood of a loyal soldier whose wife the king had stolen and whose home he had destroyed. David must first confess his sin and repent in sackcloth and ashes and then, verily, he would be heard and his prayers, as in the days of his youth when his heart was right with God, would be gloriously answered.

And so we draw out from this deep mine which we have called "the unanswered prayer" a precious lesson, which if heeded will lead us to the hidden veins of gold in the very life of God. Is my prayer life weak, and are my most earnest supplications failing to bring the desired results because of some sinful practice? Are there doubtful things in my life, grievous in the sight of God? And are these the reason for so many defeats? Have I been unwilling to make the sharp, uncompromising break with sin that is required of me in Romans six, where I am told to reckon myself to be indeed dead unto sin but alive unto God through Jesus Christ our Lord? Is not this the explanation I have long desired to have of my wretched failures as I have sought the Lord in prayer, and have come so far short of achievements such as others mighty in prayer have wrought, achievements such as a host of Biblical promises declare should be mine?

Unanswered prayers also point in the direction of cross-purposes with God. Prayer's highest function is to get us in step with the Most High. If it does not first bring us into line with the outworking of God's most holy and blessed purposes, it cannot achieve in the realms of personal desire. Paul's cry in the hour of his conversion, "Lord what would thou have me to do?" was the groundwork of a life among other things immeasurably great, that was mighty in prayer. The object of prayer is not to bend the Lord and to bring His power and wealth to the fulfillment of our own personal caprice. If there is one central thought which these chapters have aimed to lay at the foundations of this great theme, it is that prayer does not come truly into its own nor accomplish its full quota (and we have said that it is the greatest force in the universe) except it be on the basis of the Cross. It is only as with Paul I can say, "I am crucified with Christ: nevertheless I live; yet not I but Christ liveth in me," that I find solid ground for a life of prayer.

The great intercessors of the Bible were all marching in the direction of the fulfillment of the eternal purposes of God. Even the Saviour, and no one as He, must heed this law. "The Son can do nothing of himself, but what he seeth the Father do: for what things soever he doeth, these also doeth the Son likewise," was the ruling principle of His life. Only once, and then it was when He must become a curse in an identification with the sin of the world that it might be expiated, did He say, "If it be possible, let this cup pass." Ah, the real prayer was, "Not my will, but thine be done."

If we would only let God be God, which of course means a sovereign control of our lives and such a divine direction of our affairs as Jesus, the Son of Man owned, we would not have to do much asking. Our little bark would be swept along by that River of Life which proceeds from the throne and from the Lamb, and we would experience a fruition such as that which Paul had in mind when he said, "All things are yours, for ye are Christ's." Surely the psalmist was thinking of this when he said, "Delight thyself also in the Lord; and he will give thee the desires of thine heart" (Ps. 37:4). It is only when we begin to move in the direction of "self-will," which at heart is a declaration of independence as to the sovereignty of God in our human sphere, that we begin to discover a disparity, yea, a mighty difference between our meager achievements in the realm of prayer and what is represented by the promises of God.

And so we come to the second lesson to be mined from the hidden treasure of the unanswered prayer. Failure in prayer should bring me to the realization that I have not been still to listen to His voice. He wants to speak and show me what He is doing; He wants to perform all things for me, to use the language of the psalmist, but I am moving in a world of my own creation, where "self" is king. I have been busy about my own affairs. They may be good; they may even be the affairs of the Church and of missions. But I have not allowed Christ to carry the burden and to take the helm. It is when He is the Alpha and the Omega, the Soul of one's soul, the Life of one's life, the Beginning and the End of one's dreams, and His glory an all-consuming passion, that prayer becomes as natural as breathing and the results as stupendous as the promises of God and commensurate with the declarations of Holy Writ.

The unanswered prayer, too, leads to the discovery that often God wants to give us something great while we have been demanding something small. The classic illustration is Paul's prayer in II Corinthians twelve, to which we have already referred in a former chapter. Paul was sick and he asked the Lord (thrice he prayed, II Cor. 12:8) that his thorn which he calls a messenger of Satan to buffet him, might be removed. But that thorn, whatever its nature may have been (some wild guesses as to its character have been made, ranging from ophthalmia to epilepsy) was fulfilling a significant mission in the divine economy. Paul, the greatest of the apostles, a chosen vessel to bear the name which is above every name before the Gentiles and kings, the foremost maker of history, must be nothing in himself that Christ might be all and in all. He must be a corn of wheat that falls into the ground to die even as his Lord and Saviour did. He must exemplify the Cross in which he so glorified, and which he so courageously preached as to its deeper implications, namely co-crucifixion as the way out of sin and as the secret of the Christian's victory. He must be able to say and literally know the deepest depths of the meaning of such a position as, "I am crucified with Christ, nevertheless I live, and yet not I but Christ liveth in me . . . ." He must realize as no one in the great succession of the saints that "we which live are alway delivered unto death for Jesus' sake that the life also of Jesus might be made manifest in our mortal flesh." Hence the thorn in Paul's flesh. And prayer did not remove it. Supplication failed to bring the longed for results.

But that is not all. Ah, how sweet the Saviour's voice as He speaks to his afflicted servant, "My grace is sufficient for thee: for my strength is made perfect in weakness." "Paul," the thought seems to be, "the great purposes for the furtherance of the Kingdom of God which are to be realized through you, can be fulfilled in no other way. To break the power of 'the natural' so that your strength might be that power which was manifested in the resurrection of your Lord, and that you might draw moment by moment on that treasure of divine life, the thorn is necessary. Do not fear, my grace is sufficient for thee." Paul sees the Cross and the empty tomb in a new light and ceases to pray for the removal of his thorn. He is wholly reconciled to his pain and declares that he will glory in his infirmity that the power of Christ might rest upon him. What a wealth of light this sheds upon the mystery of the unanswered prayer. We ask for a penny, while the Lord aims to give us a million of an infinitely higher order.

The theology of the unanswered prayer takes us also to the consideration of the fact that often we are not in the right frame of mind to pray. We cannot understand why the heavens seem to be brass and our earnest cry of no avail, but the reason is to be found in our restless, excited, fussy state. We are in a hurry; we rush here and there; we are fretful and anxious about a thousand things. We strain over this role and now that. We are out of sorts and forever passing from one tension to another in our relation with people. We pray hard as one situation after another develops and are hurt and think of God in a faultfinding fashion because He does not seem to care, nor to hear our prayer. We criticize His providences and harbor secret doubts as to His love.

We must change our attitude. We must come to a position of rest. The psalmist understood. He gives us the key in Psalm 37:7, 8, "Rest in the Lord, and wait patiently for him: fret not thyself because of him who prospereth in his way . . . . Cease from anger and forsake wrath: fret not thyself in any wise to do evil." The Psalmist had heard the Lord say, "Be still and know that I am God." Our loving Heavenly Father cannot manifest Himself to us and work the great and mighty things He would in our behalf until we settle down to a restful position before Him. It is the high and holy function of the Cross to bring this to pass. The fussy, restless, excited, ever-straining and never fully attaining "self-life" which keeps you out of step with God, was in His divine economy crucified together with Christ. With Him you were raised and made to sit together with Him in heavenly places. You must enter in by faith. When you do, learning to rest in the Lord and to let Him take the lead, your prayers will become a chain of miracles, never ending, forever achieving in the might of the Spirit of God, and you will stand speechless in the presence of the Most High, worshiping in immeasurable awe and wonder. It will be with you as it was with those to whom the Lord referred when He said, ". . . before they call, I will answer" (Isa. 65:24).

The "Why" of the unanswered prayer also takes us to another thought. It may be as it was in the case of Job, that the Lord is seeking to bring us to His very own self. Job had to be stripped; he had to be brought to the end of himself; he had to die as it were, before he could say, "I have heard of thee by the hearing of the ear; *but now mine eye seeth thee.* Wherefore I abhor myself and repent in dust and ashes." It was not until he ceased praying for himself and gave himself to prayer for his friends (these "friends" who had so tormented him with their insinuations that all these troubles which had come upon him were the result of some secret sin he must "confess" and all would be well)—it was not, I repeat, until he had come completely out of himself praying for these who had so wronged him, that the Lord turned his captivity (see Job 42:10).

We pray for many things, all more or less good, but God wants to give us the *summum bonum*, namely, Himself. Oh, to bring us to Himself! There was no other way but the Cross. Our old man was crucified with Him (Christ) that the body of sin might be destroyed (Rom. 6:6). We have been raised up together with Him and made to sit together with Him in heavenly places (Eph. 2:5, 6). Thus are we brought into deepest intimacy with God and made one with Him. We read that on the Mount of Transfiguration, the disciples saw no man (they had been looking at Moses and Elijah) save Jesus alone. It is good beyond measure that God does not always give us the things we ask for, that in our desperation we may get beyond "things" and cease to pray for mere "blessings," in order to get to God Himself and rest in Him alone. In having Him, we have all.

A closing word is in order to those who mourn because they feel that God has let them down. Their most cherished hope has long been deferred. They cry in vain, but the Lord, so it seems, turns to them a deaf ear. Years have gone by, yet their earnest supplication for some dear one that the Lord might bring him to a knowledge of Himself has gone unheeded. They cannot understand why others seem to get everything they ask for, while they plead their cause before the throne of grace to no avail. For such, I have a blessed word of hope and cheer in the fact that God's delays are not denials. They form a necessary part of the discipline of faith. He means for us to hold on even though there be no star of hope in the night of our pain. George Müller prayed for over forty years for the conversion of two dear friends. He was chided by one who said to him, "Mr. Müller, you say that all your prayers are answered. What do you mean?"

The reply was, "I have prayed for many years for the Lord to bring two I dearly love to Himself. They have not yet accepted Christ as their Saviour. But I know that they eventually will come to know Him. Therefore I say, 'all my prayers are answered.'" Not long after, George Müller saw these for whom he had so long interceded, surrender to Christ and confess His Name. Faith sorely tried won out.

So we must not give up. The widow of the parable did not give up. The unjust judge before whom she pleaded her cause is described as a hard worldling who feared not God neither regarded man, in order to accentuate by contrast the goodness of God. The thought is that if a wicked judge finally gives in to a grief-stricken widow so that she might not weary him by her continual coming, how much more must a loving Heavenly Father, whose mercy cannot be measured, respond to those who call upon Him according to the needs and desires of their hearts. No, we must not give up. The answer when it comes will be all the sweeter. The blessing when it comes will be all the greater. The joy will be all the more unspeakable, and the praise offered in return, all the more jubilant and sincere. Faith only comes to be true faith after it has been tried. You have prayed for years for something that you desire more than life. You shall have the desire of your heart, and you will have all eternity to praise the Lord for His faithfulness.

When Daniel prayed for his people, the children of Israel, that they might be delivered from their captivity, the angel Gabriel sent to strengthen him said to him, "Fear not, Daniel: for from the first day that thou didst set thine heart to understand and to chasten thyself before thy God, thy words were heard . . . But the prince of the kingdom of Persia withstood me one and twenty days; but, lo,

Michael, one of the chief princes came to help me . . . Now
I am come to make thee understand what shall befall thy
people in the latter days." What a lesson here for discouraged intercessors! Daniel's prayer was heard from the
first. But the "powers of darkness" had interfered. The
delay was from the "pit," not from heaven. Gabriel and
his aides had to fight it out with the prince of darkness
before the answer could come. All hell moves against the
prayers of the saints, but let them be of good cheer. The
prince of this world is a defeated foe (see Heb. 2:14 and
Col. 2:14, 15). He must give way before the victory of
Calvary to which Christians testify. The gates of hell
shall not prevail. Christians are more than conquerors
through Him who loved them. No true believer has ever
been "let down" by the Great Shepherd of the sheep. If
they will but hold on in prayer, victory is as sure as the
rising of the sun. Only let them not faint. God's time
is best. Prayer warrior, do not give up the fight. Your
prayer was heard from the first, as it was with Daniel.
Let not contrary winds discourage thee. For you, too,
is the word which came to the prophet; it is for all intercessors, "At the beginning of thy supplications the com-
mandment came forth, and I am come to shew thee! for
thou art greatly beloved" (Dan 9:23).